Living Abstinent

Living Abstinent

GreySheeters Anonymous

Greysheeters Anonymous Conference Approved Literature. This literature has been approved at a GSA World Service Conference and is consistent with the Twelve Steps, Twelve Traditions, and Twelve Concepts of Greysheeters Anonymous.

Print information available on the last page.

Rev. date: 04/19/2021

To order additional copies of this book, contact:
Xlibris
844-714-8691
www.Xlibris.com
Orders@Xlibris.com
807489

CONTENTS

Slogans to Live By

Life in GSA Recovery

This book is dedicated to all those who seek abstinence and recovery from food addiction through the GreySheet solution.

The only relief we have to suggest
is entire abstinence.

Alcoholics Anonymous, *Alcoholics Anonymous,* xxviii

Introduction

In 1975, Alcoholics Anonymous published a book called *Living Sober*. In it, many alcoholics shared how they stayed sober. Staying sober, after all, is the basis of recovery from alcoholism. Most of us in GreySheeters Anonymous (GSA) agree with the premise that the basis of our recovery from food addiction is learning how to live without bingeing, starving, grazing, or whatever form of abuse our eating took. Using *Living Sober* as a guide to living in recovery, we have put together our own book called *Living Abstinent*.

Our primary purpose in GSA is first to abstain from compulsive eating, and next to give service to the fellowship, and carry the message of recovery to compulsive eaters who still suffer. This book emphasizes the first aspect of our primary purpose, getting and staying abstinent. In the first couple of years of a GreySheeter's recovery, the practical aspects of abstinence became our focus. For most of us, it was like learning a new language. It was hard work and took a lot of practice every day. Sometimes we had to avoid places that had foods that we were addicted to. We had to learn how to shop in grocery stores, how to stick to a shopping list, how to deal with parties and buffet dinners, how to live with people who loved us, but didn't understand the extreme nature of our disease, and much, much more.

We have broken this book down into chapters that address many issues. Some of the topics are particularly helpful for someone who is new to GSA, and other topics are useful for both newcomers and those with many years of GreySheet abstinence. We have reached out to long-time GSA members for their experience. What you will read in the following chapters is the gathered experience, strength, and hope shared in meetings, or written to us at our request.

Most of us have found that over time, addressing everyday problems related to our abstinence becomes second nature to us. Living abstinently is not a restriction or a sacrifice. Not only can we enjoy special occasions, we can enjoy life in general. We no longer focus on how to get our "fix," but on the company we keep. We have a new curiosity about people, and about life. We have begun to realize that there is no limit to our growth and learning. It is up to us. We are each different, and we all have the chance to find ourselves, and turn to whatever sources attract us as we grow.

What we have in common is the life and death disease of compulsive eating, or food addiction. We have experienced living in the hell of eating compulsively. We will go to any lengths to help each other never to have to return to that hell. This book offers specific guidance for GSA members who want to stay abstinent. We want to share all of this with you.

NOTE: We value your experiences with GreySheet abstinence. We welcome your feedback on this book, including adding to the editors' ideas for future chapters. Please send any input to: literature@greysheet.org ("ATT: Living Abstinent" in the subject line).

What You Will Find in This Book

This book presents what has helped members of GreySheeters Anonymous to *get through everyday life experiences and situations abstinently*—putting abstinence first, no matter what else happens in our lives. We provide practical information about the people and practices that support our abstinence. We share about how we got through particular challenges in early abstinence. We share experience on negotiating relationships with the people in our lives, once we've stopped eating compulsively. We discuss managing our emotions and thoughts in ways that best support our ongoing abstinence. We address common issues that recovering compulsive eaters face. In essence, we offer many of the strategies and tools that have been the most helpful in maintaining our abstinence. Read this book alone, with your sponsor, or in a literature meeting where you can hear other members share their own experiences with all of these topics. Let us know what you think.

This book will *not* give you a food plan. We get the GreySheet along with our choice of a sponsor. Our sponsor discusses with us everything that is written on the GreySheet. This book does *not* give instructions on how to work the Twelve Steps of GreySheeters Anonymous, or how to interpret them. Both Alcoholics Anonymous and GreySheeters Anonymous provide literature on the Steps (see "Appendix: Literature"). And this book does not include every topic that GSA members discuss together. It is not meant to take the place of members reaching out to their sponsors and other GreySheeters to ask questions, share experience, and build fellowship—but rather to support conversation and open doors to the exchange of ideas and the experience of others.

Once we are abstinent, most of us find that certain long-held behaviors and thoughts can trigger us to want to eat compulsively. We realize that if we want to stay abstinent, we must change these behavioral and thinking patterns. We change over time by working the Twelve Steps, attending GSA meetings, using the tools we share in this book, and getting help outside of GSA when we need it.

As we have more days of abstinence behind us, we experience more freedom from food—from the physical cravings and mental obsession. Most of us begin to have full lives that contain work, families, and hobbies. Sometimes we need help with difficulties in these areas as they relate to our abstinence. None of us wants to feel that our abstinence is being threatened. We need to learn what to do, and what *not* to do. This book offers strategies for dealing with situations that we weren't able to negotiate successfully in the past, and suggestions for situations to avoid, in order to protect our abstinence. These are strategies that help us at home and at work, while alone and at social events, in our local community and while traveling. They guide us in staying abstinent now, and in all of the life situations to come.

Each of us has to learn what works for us, to fill our own "toolbox" with what aids us to plan, prepare, and protect our abstinence. No two toolboxes will be identical. Here we offer as many tools as we can. Take what you need and leave the rest. We encourage you to keep an open mind as you read this book. Suggestions may seem strange at first and you might not be able to imagine getting abstinent. But you won't know if these suggestions will work for you if you don't try them. Most of us found that our own best ideas about how to manage our eating eventually led us to GreySheeters Anonymous. Our own ideas didn't work.

There is some common advice for newcomers from all of the members who contributed to this book: stick very close to your sponsor and follow directions, especially about the mechanics of following the GreySheet food plan; call three abstinent GreySheeters per day and ask them how they stayed abstinent through difficult situations; go to meetings. And keep talking. Talk to your sponsor, talk to your new GSA friends, and talk at meetings. This will help you be a part of the GreySheeters Anonymous fellowship.

Compulsive eating is a cunning disease. We have found that we need to work our programs and use our tools vigilantly to build a defense against eating compulsively again. So be smart in taking suggestions about how to "fill up" your toolbox. And join us in our new way of life—a life without eating compulsively no matter what, one day at a time. In other words, an abstinent life.

Note to readers regarding the use of the pronoun "they" in reference to an individual person: in some instances, the gender of the contributing GSA member was unknown to the authors, or not relevant in that message of recovery. In other instances, a member may have requested gender-neutral pronouns. This is all in accordance with the current *Chicago Manual of Style*.

12 steps
meetings
tools - toolbox
outside help.
plan, prepare, protect,
keep an open mind

Beginning Our GSA Journey

1

Abstinence

"The only relief we have to suggest is entire abstinence."[1] So says *Alcoholics Anonymous*, the primary text of A.A. (generally called the Big Book).

We are compulsive eaters and food addicts, but we must eat. As GreySheeters, we abstain entirely from all forms of sugar, grains, and starchy carbohydrates, because these foods are our drug. We do not eat anything that is not on the GreySheet. On our food plan, we weigh and measure three meals a day with nothing in between but black coffee, tea, diet soda, and water. *Entire abstinence* means we don't eat in between meals—ever. When we first come to GSA, it can be challenging for some of us to eat only three times a day, but we get used to this new way of eating.

Any newcomer to a GSA meeting who asks for a copy of our food plan is told that the GreySheet comes with a sponsor. For a true compulsive eater, the GreySheet food plan is not enough on its own. To attain GreySheet abstinence, newcomers need to find a qualified sponsor (someone with at least ninety days of back-to-back GreySheet abstinence) and then follow their directions. Our sponsor will give us a copy of the GreySheet. At the start, our sponsor works with us,

---

[1]   Alcoholics Anonymous, *Alcoholics Anonymous,* Fourth Edition (New York: Alcoholics Anonymous World Services, Inc, 2001), xxviii.

either in person or over the phone, to explain the specifics of weighing and measuring our food from the GreySheet. As our sponsor reviews the GreySheet with us in detail, we find it helpful to take notes, either directly on our GreySheet or on a separate piece of paper. We might keep our annotated GreySheet and other notes in the kitchen to refer to. When we call to commit our food to our sponsor each day, we ask questions about anything we're unsure about. We follow the slogan that appears on the GreySheet, When in Doubt, Leave It Out, until we have checked with our sponsor. Sponsors give us specific and ongoing guidance for maintaining our abstinence.

While some GreySheeters work with the same sponsor for years, we are free to change sponsors if we need to. Sometimes our schedule changes and we're not able to commit our food when our sponsor is available. Or it may become clear that our sponsor is no longer a good fit for some other reason. Over time, members gain clarity about what they need in a sponsor. One member shared that she needs a sponsor who supports her in keeping her food simple, and answers the phone when she calls.

In addition to what is written on the GreySheet, there are certain guidelines that are part of our abstinence. We leave at least four hours between meals. We do not eat before 6:00 a.m. or after midnight. We work with our sponsors when there are special circumstances in our lives that affect the timing of our meals on a regular basis, or when a situation requires exceptional planning.

In early abstinence we learn how to prepare our abstinent food, and we are vigilant when making our meals. Even so, sometimes we make mistakes. For example, we might drop a portion of our weighed and measured meal onto a dirty floor. Or we might finish eating a meal, and later realize that we left a portion of it sitting in the microwave. We could give other examples. An essential part of maintaining our abstinence is that we *never* make independent food decisions.

In those cases, we always call our own sponsor or another qualified GreySheet food sponsor. We let that person tell us what to do. Our telephone is one of the most important tools for maintaining our abstinence. In addition to taking our calls when we need immediate support, our sponsor can help us develop useful strategies based on our particular challenges—for example, checking our meal against our written food plan before we sit down to eat, to make sure we have not omitted anything.

All of the guidelines of our food plan provide the foundation of our GreySheet abstinence, and help to keep us safe from sliding back into compulsive eating. For most of us, the guidelines also halt the mental obsession that is part of food addiction. We may have obsessed about getting food, stopping ourselves from getting food, and about the type and quantity of food we ate. In GSA we know exactly what we eat every day, which gives us mental peace.

The purpose of this book is to help you maintain abstinence. Although we don't discuss these instances in every chapter, we acknowledge that some of us struggled to get abstinent in the first place, or to maintain back-to-back abstinence. It took some of us time before we grasped the idea of surrender, accepted our powerlessness over our disease, and were willing to go to any lengths to be abstinent. To those who struggle, we encourage you to keep using the GreySheet food plan and every program tool available. Keep coming back to meetings and to connection with other GreySheeters. When you keep coming back, you're better able to hear what you need to do to get and stay abstinent. We believe that all members can have continuous GreySheet abstinence if we remain willing to go to any lengths to keep it. We can have that miracle if we 100% surrender to our powerlessness over food. In this book, when we speak about "our" abstinence, we are speaking about your abstinence, too, even if you're not there yet.

In the following chapters, experienced GreySheeters share helpful suggestions on how to maintain long-term abstinence. Although following the GreySheet food plan may feel strange and difficult in the beginning, for many hundreds of grateful compulsive eaters, GreySheet abstinence has become a way of life, making life worth living.

No matter if we've reached a normal weight, or attained a period of abstinence, we must never forget the deadly nature of our disease. But we can experience a balance between a healthy fear of our disease, and the peace and safety we have when we are abstinent.

We are taught that if we work our program every day, we have a twenty-four-hour reprieve from compulsive eating. We do exactly what we have been doing since day one. We continue to call other GreySheeters and go to meetings. We plan and prepare our food each day. We do service in our fellowship. In exchange, we have twenty-four hours of freedom from our disease. We no longer battle the urge to eat compulsively. We never again have to live in fear of food.

When we remember that we are compulsive eaters with the *gift* of abstinence, and work every day to protect this gift, we walk a path that we couldn't dream of when we were eating compulsively. One member of our GSA community shares, "Eating abundant, satisfying meals has replaced the nausea and numbness of compulsive eating." Another member says, "Compulsive eating is a slow death. Abstinence is hope and life."

Let us join together on the journey of abstinence, one day at a time.

2

Getting Through Withdrawal

According to the Big Book of Alcoholics Anonymous, the effect of alcohol on alcoholics is a symptom of an allergy. Sugar and grains are the ingredients in alcohol, and in GreySheeters Anonymous, we learn that we are compulsive eaters who are allergic to these foods in the same way that alcoholics are allergic to alcohol. We also learn that we're addicted to these substances. When we eat them, they trigger a mental obsession, plus a physical craving for more.

When we follow the GreySheet food plan, we abstain from sugar, grains, and starchy or refined carbohydrates. We may understand that we're addicted to these foods, but we might not expect that we'll suffer withdrawal symptoms when we first get abstinent and no longer eat them. When alcoholics stop drinking and are going through detox—whether at home, in rehab, or at the hospital—they generally do very little but rest, and focus completely on their recovery. We have something to learn from them. A long-time GreySheeter says:

> My sponsor told me that food addiction is one of the hardest addictions to withdraw from. Alcoholics and drug addicts who are hospitalized are in their bedroom slippers for thirty days while they detox, before they graduate to a halfway house. Yet some new GreySheeters think they can

> *continue doing their usual crazy lives while going through*
> *withdrawal, learning to be abstinent, and establishing a*
> *new way of living. Wear your figurative bedroom slippers*
> *for at least the first thirty days.*

The hallmark of mental and physical withdrawal is the craving for food. For some of us, food cravings are lifted immediately, once we become abstinent. But many of us continue to have cravings for some time. This can feel overwhelming. As we stay abstinent and eat only our three GreySheet meals each day, these powerful cravings can come and go. After a few weeks, our cravings tend to subside and we begin to feel the freedom that comes from not eating our addictive substances.

Other physical withdrawal symptoms vary in intensity for each person; some members may simply have headaches and feel tired. Symptoms might also include sore muscles, deep fatigue, the sweats, nausea, diarrhea, or constipation. Our bodies are going through a significant change. When we take away foods that our bodies have gotten used to living on, for some of us, it may feel like every part of us is crying out in misery. A long-timer shares, "My withdrawal was dramatic. Getting abstinent was a huge shock to my system. Experienced GreySheeters told me I was going through detox."

It's important that sponsors tell their newly abstinent sponsees that going through withdrawal is normal, even if it's very uncomfortable. To some newcomers, withdrawal may feel like a physical illness that needs to be treated by a medical professional. Sponsors may be able to help differentiate the symptoms of withdrawal (like fatigue, headaches, and digestive issues) from actual illness. They can reassure and advise their sponsees.

We are recovering from years of self-abuse. We consider seriously what we did to our bodies when we were active in our addiction. For years we abused ourselves by bingeing, fasting, dieting, vomiting and/or using laxatives, and over-exercising. Some of us gained and lost hundreds of pounds—and we often repeated that cycle over and over again. Some of us who vomited injured our esophagus and destroyed our tooth enamel. When we overused laxatives, we put stress on our digestive system. Human bodies aren't designed to withstand frequent vomiting, excessive exercise or laxative use, or repeated, large weight fluctuations.

As we stay abstinent, our bodies heal and get back into balance, and our physical symptoms diminish.

Many of us come into the program with full or part-time jobs, families, and other responsibilities. It's recommended that we cut out all but what is absolutely necessary in early abstinence.

As we're going through withdrawal, we are advised to rest, keep life as simple as we can, focus our energy on the basics of our GSA program, and take extra good care of ourselves.

Our sponsors, and those who have gone before us, tell us to stick close to the program. They advise us to go to as many meetings as possible, which isn't difficult in this era of phone and video meetings. In addition to attending meetings, we focus on talking to other GreySheeters, preparing our food, and learning to enjoy our meals. For the sake of efficiency, we can combine doing an important task with getting an infusion of program support. For example, some of us prepare food while listening to member shares from the GSA channel on YouTube. We get to hear the GSA message, and remember what is important.

We have many suggestions for ways of taking care of yourself during this time of detox. Read a book you've been waiting to read for a long time. Take a long bath. Go out for a walk or a hike (and perhaps invite another GreySheeter along). Watch a movie. If we feel anxious, we can do chores that use up nervous energy. On the other hand, we shouldn't overdo; it's sensible to take a break whenever we feel tired.

Talk to your sponsor and to other GreySheeters about what you're going through in your withdrawal process. We are told early on that this is a "we" program, and that we never again have to do anything alone. One member says, "I was advised to tell my sponsor exactly what I was feeling, and also to share at meetings. People told me the same thing had happened to them and that they survived it." Another member went to a retreat with her sponsor when she had one month of abstinence.

"It was amazing to weigh and measure my food with all of those other GreySheeters. Even though I was extremely tired, I also felt so happy, so 'un-alone.' I couldn't have done anything better for myself in early abstinence. I'm so glad my sponsor talked me into going."

As our bodies detox physically, the withdrawal process also includes our emotions. Many of us believe that our emotional growth was interrupted when we started eating compulsively, and that we never learned to deal with our feelings in a healthy way. Now that we're abstinent, our emotions can feel overpowering.

In addition, it's likely that we were mentally and emotionally reliant on food in order to cope with the challenges in our lives. For many of us, those challenges involved our human relationships; when we ate compulsively, we may have lacked the ability to cope with the stresses of those relationships in healthy ways.

During early abstinence and withdrawal, it may feel difficult when we begin to form or rebuild relationships with others. One member relates that she was fifty years old when she first got abstinent, but she felt like she was twelve. Learning how to be in mature relationships started with her relationship with her sponsor. "I had to learn to trust my sponsor. I had never trusted anyone in my life, and friends were pulling away from me. I thought other people were the cause of all my problems. Emotionally, I had a lot to learn. It wasn't easy, but the rewards are worth it a hundred times over."

In GSA, we are told that in our recovery from compulsive eating we work to change our old ways of thinking, feeling, and behaving when we are uncomfortable or distressed. In order to do this work, we need the clarity that abstinence gives us. And in order to be abstinent, we need to go through the withdrawal process. Our sponsors and the GSA community are there to help us along the way. One member says, "Be gentle with yourself. You are asking your body, mind, and spirit to do an extraordinary thing—to function without the crutch of food."

For many of us, going through withdrawal was one of the hardest things we ever did. In our experience, there is no way *around* withdrawal. If we want to be free from our compulsion, the only way is to go *through* it. Abstinent members remind us that this difficult time passes. Withdrawal does end and, as we stay abstinent one day at a time, we never have to go through it again. And we are not alone on this part of our abstinent journey.

3

Going to Meetings

When we first connected with members of Greysheeters Anonymous, whether by phone, by email, through the website, or by showing up at a meeting, we were told that attending meetings regularly is the most important support for our abstinence.

Some of us had a sponsor who required that we go to at least one meeting per day during our first ninety days in GSA. For many of us, this seemed like a lot for our sponsor to ask of us. We had jobs, families, and other responsibilities that took up time in our lives. Why were meetings so important? How could we possibly fit in all the meetings we were being asked to attend?

A member of GSA said, "When I was newly abstinent, I was told I had to 'have my brain washed.' My sponsor told me to go to as many meetings as I possibly could and surround myself with the GSA message of recovery." That's what the sponsor had been told to do, so she passed this guidance on to her sponsee.

In order to build a defense against eating compulsively again, we have to be constantly reminded of what our life was like before we got abstinent. And the "disease thoughts" we have had most of our lives must be replaced, day after day, with "recovery thoughts." That's what happens at meetings.

Even after we reach ninety days of abstinence, most of us choose to attend GSA meetings frequently. Most sponsors are likely to suggest a minimum of three meetings a week. Some GreySheeters attend a meeting every day, whenever they can.

In addition, meetings give us the opportunity to do service, which is one of the most important ways that we participate in GSA. We break the isolation that is at the core of addiction. We are connected and accountable to other recovering compulsive eaters. We contribute to others' recovery, and to keeping GSA going. We express gratitude to the fellowship that saves our lives on a daily basis, and don't take it for granted.

Early in abstinence, we might feel shy about getting involved at meetings. But even volunteering to do readings or time members' shares is a contribution, and it gets us outside of ourselves. Once we have ninety days of back-to-back GreySheet abstinence, we are qualified to sponsor, lead or share our story at meetings, book speakers, be a treasurer, or take on a number of other service positions. And whether we are newcomers or long-timers, just showing up abstinent at our meetings is a very important service.

One member shares that she was isolated before she came to GSA. She was unable to stop eating, and the voices in her head told her that food was the answer to all of her problems. In GSA, she learned that the antidote to isolation was to put herself "in the middle of the herd"—to get involved. She was told,

> Go to meetings: in-person meetings, video meetings, phone meetings. Go where you can hear the solution. And between meetings, have one-on-one phone calls with other GreySheeters. You are not alone with this disease and you do not have to do this by yourself.

She listened to her sponsor and followed directions, and today this member has almost thirty years of back-to-back GreySheet abstinence.

Newcomers sometimes resist going to meetings, and say to their sponsor: "Ok, I'll go to meetings as you suggest. But how long do I have to keep going?" A wise sponsor will say: "Keep going until you *want* to go!" One sponsor explains to her sponsee just how much GSA meetings have come to mean to her:

> *The GreySheeters at my meetings are my community. All I have to say is I'm a compulsive eater, and they recognize the deepest truth about me. These people understand me. All my life I've wanted to be understood. Over the years, I've changed the meetings I go to as my life has changed, but I always have a home group—a place I can be heard and a place where I'll be missed if I'm not there.*

A member with many years of abstinence shares:

> *Once I got ninety days, I started telling my story at meetings. I talked about my last binge and how I got to GSA, and what drove me to such desperation that I was finally willing to do what I was told to do by the members who came before me. Today, I go to hear others tell their stories. I want to be reminded over and over again about the hell of being face down in the food. I never want to go back there. And by attending a meeting, I'm doing service by carrying the message to other compulsive eaters, and helping to make sure that GSA is there for the newcomer. Going to meetings is one of the most powerful tools I have to protect me from that first compulsive bite.*

What if I live in an outpost?

Some long-timers started their GSA program living in an "outpost" (here we're defining an outpost as a place that's more than three hours of travel from an in-person meeting). They worried that they wouldn't be able to stay abstinent. A few of these members traveled to the "hubs" of GSA (Cambridge, MA and New York City, NY at the time), and went to as many meetings as were available during their visits. Several members actually relocated, either temporarily or permanently, so they could be near GSA meetings.

But not all of us were able do that. One long-timer asked her sponsor: "What should I do? There aren't any meetings near me, and I can't drive two hours to get to one." She was advised to attend as many A.A. meetings as she could find in her area, and to stay in touch daily with GreySheeters by phone and by letter.

Today, we can participate in phone meetings via conference call companies (the schedule is at www.greysheet.org). There are as many as twelve phone meetings per day: speaker (qualification) meetings, women's meetings, men's meetings, and slogan meetings, among others. At these meetings we can get the phone numbers of other members. Some of us have gotten abstinent on the GreySheet without ever having met another GreySheeter in person!

We can also participate in video conference meetings on the internet, where we can see our GSA brothers and sisters. Every GSA Intergroup hosts many video meetings per week (the schedule is at www.greysheet. org). Look for the days and times that work for you. One member told us,

> My Zoom meeting is my home group. I depend on seeing the same people week after week. They are my neighbors. I know I'm never alone with this horrible disease when I see their smiling faces and know that they're doing what I am doing.

What if I want to start an in-person meeting?

Any abstinent GreySheeter can start an in-person meeting if they want to build or expand a local GSA community. If possible, it's sensible to do this with a GSA friend, but many of us have started meetings by ourselves and waited patiently as the meeting attracted new people and grew larger as the weeks and months went by. We need only find a place to hold the meeting (for example, a church or community center where other Twelve-Step meetings are already held).

Then we put the word out to the GSA fellowship. We make sure the new meeting is included in the list of meetings on the GSA website, and on GreyNet, an online forum for GSA members (for access to this platform, ask your sponsor or go to www.greysheet.org). We can also announce the new meeting on phone and video meetings, and via social media. In order to let members of our local community know about the meeting, some of us put notices in the local newspaper. The www. greysheet.org website has a page called "How to Start a GSA Meeting Near You." Here you will find detailed information, and access to brochures, cards, and leaflets you can pass out to friends, doctors, teachers, and other professionals to help spread the word.

One of our members shared,

> *I went to a church that hosted Alcoholics Anonymous meetings. I told them what I wanted to do, but that I had no money to pay rent. They kindly told me not to worry, that I should get the meeting going and once people were coming regularly, then I could make a regular donation to the church. That's exactly what happened.*

Another member tells us that she started a meeting in the United Kingdom. For the first six weeks she was the only person to show up, so she decided to sit there and read out of the Big Book of Alcoholics Anonymous. She had read the entire book by the time a second person finally came to the meeting. She said, "I never would have read that book if I hadn't decided to start a meeting. Now we are a literature meeting, and everyone gets to read the Big Book with me."

Don't be discouraged if you start a meeting that doesn't survive. This sometimes happens. We can try our best, but it doesn't always work out. A long-time GreySheeter shares that she started several meetings over the years, that for one reason or another did not last. Luckily, there are many thriving meetings for us to participate in.

Whatever meetings we attend, whether in-person or virtual, we will hear the message of GSA abstinence. GreySheeters Anonymous meetings are central in our recovery from compulsive eating. At meetings, we build lasting connections with other GreySheeters, so that we aren't alone with our disease or our recovery. We hear members' stories that remind us of how devastating food addiction is; and we also immerse ourselves in stories of recovery. And we are doing important service for the community just by being there. We strengthen our own abstinence by supporting the meeting, helping GSA to thrive so that we are here for other compulsive eaters. Meetings are our lifeline, our community, and our home.

4

Making Phone Calls

Go to meetings—Check.
Call your sponsor—Check.
Weigh and measure your food—Check.
Never eat between meals—Check.
Call three GreySheeters a day.…

That last suggestion seemed the hardest to some of us. Many long-term members remember that, in early abstinence, this felt almost impossible.

Most of us come into the rooms of GreySheeters Anonymous feeling bad about ourselves-—hopeless about climbing out of the hole we are in with food. We are full of shame, confusion, remorse, and self-hatred. We may be afraid of others' opinions. We want to do what we are told by our sponsor, but we may not be able to imagine calling any of the people we see or hear at meetings who are actually abstinent. Just thinking about making a phone call to someone we don't know might make us very nervous. What if they hang up on us? What if we leave a message that sounds stupid? We may be afraid we'll embarrass ourselves. We may wonder what we possibly have to offer, anyway.

If we are anxious about making phone calls to other GreySheeters, our sponsors tell us not to worry. They say that the more calls we make, the more comfortable we will feel doing so. They tell us that when we call other GreySheeters, we can ask questions, get support, and build relationships. Making phone calls is another tool in our kit for attaining and maintaining GreySheet abstinence. It's another action we can take to strengthen our commitment, one day at a time.

One member who was particularly shy when she came into the program recalls that when she was eating compulsively, she lived a life of secrecy and isolation. By going to meetings, she no longer had to be alone. But it could still be tempting to sit in the back of the room and avoid talking to anyone. Making three phone calls a day, she got to know the people at the meetings and benefited from the experience, strength, and hope of many more abstinent members. Instead of feeling "apart from" as she had in the past, she felt "a part of." She often found that other GreySheeters had the information she needed. She received help, and even friendship. And as she came to feel that she belonged, it became easier to volunteer to do service for the meeting. In turn, doing service increased her feeling of belonging to the group.

Over time, she became grateful for the connections she was making by calling other GreySheeters. There was always someone there to take a food change, offer help in the case of a food mistake or emergency, or listen if she was having the kind of hard day that used to lead to eating compulsively.

Another member describes her experience with phone calls this way:

> For me, making phone calls builds a good foundation for recovery, and is great training for reaching out to others. Staying in contact with other GreySheeters gives me a lifeline when I can't reach my sponsor in a food emergency. And I am much more likely to pick up the phone before picking up the food, if I have established connections with other GreySheeters.

A long-time abstinent member shares:

> Three phone calls a day is the minimum that was recommended to me. I was told that the people who give

out their phone numbers do so because they're willing to take calls from other GreySheeters. These calls can be simple. We can just say that we are powerless over food, that we're abstinent and weighing and measuring three meals from the GreySheet today, and that we are grateful. A short call can take thirty seconds. And by calling another GreySheeter we are actually doing service. The person we call is the recipient of our GreySheet abstinent message. So we are helping others and ourselves at the same time. Phone calls make a huge difference in our feeling of belonging to the program and having the support we need.

Those who have a long list of GreySheeters' phone numbers and make a lot of phone calls are more likely to get abstinent and stay abstinent.

Nuts and Bolts of
GreySheet Abstinence

5

A Roadmap for Grocery Shopping

For most GSA members, regular trips to the grocery store are part of our lives in abstinence. Some of us enjoy grocery shopping, some of us resist doing it, and some of us need to relearn how to do it now that we are no longer eating compulsively. When we're newly abstinent, a grocery store can seem like a danger zone, filled with foods that we no longer eat. From both a practical and emotional point of view, it can be very challenging. Even long-time GSA members sometimes feel nervous when surrounded by non-abstinent foods.

GSA members share tips about finding the support we need, preparing for our trips to the grocery store, protecting our serenity and our abstinence while we're there, and making food shopping enjoyable.

Getting support

In early abstinence, one member was lucky enough to have a more experienced GreySheeter accompany them to the grocery store. If we are part of an in-person GSA community, we can ask a fellow member along. We might also invite a close friend or family member to join us.

Not every newcomer is able to bring a GreySheeter, a friend, or a family member along for a shopping trip, but we can all make phone calls in order to find support. One GreySheeter safeguarded their early abstinence this way: "When I went food shopping, I 'bookended' my trip to the store with a phone call before and after." Knowing that they would report any anxiety or temptation they felt helped to keep them grounded and on task.

Long-time GSA members can benefit from having a family member help with the shopping, especially when we need to buy non-GreySheet foods.

> *Not everything I purchase is abstinent food. I am responsible for shopping for my family and I must be very careful to avoid 'romancing' foods we do not eat. If possible, I bring a family member along to help get the job done. Incidentally, as time goes on, my family eats more and more meals that are abstinent. I prepare delicious meals for the whole family from foods on the GreySheet, and everyone is happy and well fed.*

Preparing

Many long-timers believe that making a grocery list before going shopping is essential. Planning menus ahead of time can make it easier to put grocery lists together. In addition to a list, it's wise to bring a copy of the GreySheet, our phone, and the phone numbers of our sponsor and other GSA members, in case we have questions or concerns.

One GreySheeter checks her frame of mind before going shopping to avoid being tired or hungry in the grocery store. Another member sometimes resists food shopping when she'd rather be doing something else. At these times, she calls a GSA friend. She says, "I need to go grocery shopping, but I don't want to. I'm remembering that you do what I do with food, and I'm remembering how precious our GreySheet abstinence is." This always seems to give her the motivation to get to the store.

At the store

In most chain grocery stores, the foods we eat are found on the outside aisles. Sticking to the "outside track" can keep us feeling safe and serene when we're newly abstinent. If our favorite store doesn't have this layout, we can learn which aisles to ignore. If we do need to go down aisles where non-abstinent foods are concentrated, we simply find the items on our list, and leave the aisle.

In order to avoid painful memories, one GreySheeter said goodbye to the store where he shopped when he ate compulsively, and chose a new store. Before his first shopping trip there, he toured the store with notebook in hand and recorded the locations of all the items he would need. When he returned, he was able to home in on those areas. Another member puts "blinders" on by looking straight ahead when she passes foods that are not on the GreySheet. She reminds herself that these foods are not hers. She knows the exact aisles where she'll find the items she needs, and she sticks to her grocery list.

Protecting our abstinence includes carefully reading the labels on the foods we buy, even if we've purchased those foods before. A member explains, "I read the label every time I purchase an item, because sometimes ingredients change."

If we're confused about whether something is abstinent, we call our own sponsor or another qualified GreySheet sponsor. If we don't reach anyone before we leave the store, we can leave the item behind. If we purchase it, we don't eat it unless we find out that it's abstinent.

Enjoying the trip

In GreySheeters Anonymous we often talk about buying "the biggest and the best," especially in relation to our delicious fruits and vegetables. One member is so enthusiastic about the produce they buy that they take pictures of it to send to GSA friends. "Some people share pictures of their family, but I like to share pictures of my beautiful produce!"

Practicing gratitude almost always increases the satisfaction and joy we feel, including when we're grocery shopping. We can deeply appreciate our access to abstinent food, and our ability to buy it. We can be thankful that we are able to be in a grocery store without bingeing. We can bring to mind the wonderful companionship we share with our fellow GreySheeters. And we can celebrate the extraordinary gift of abstinence, knowing that grocery shopping provides us with the foods that make up our meal plan.

6

What Is Backup?

One of our GreySheeters Anonymous slogans is There's Always a Way to Stay Abstinent. Preparing backup meals helps us to do so. In GSA we explain backup as "Taking a sufficient supply of abstinent food with us wherever we go in case we cannot get the food we need in order to stay abstinent."[2] This vital practice is the backbone of the Four Ps: Pray, Plan, Prepare, and Protect. We define the Four Ps as "Looking ahead to potential obstacles to maintaining our abstinence and finding ways to overcome them before they happen."[3] Having backup food with us is one of the most important ways that we overcome possible obstacles.

Many of us are away from home for extended periods of time during the day, or we frequently dine in restaurants or at the homes of friends, or we travel for professional or personal reasons. In some of these cases, we bring pre-weighed and measured backup meals. At other times we don't weigh and measure all of our food ahead of time, but we do bring the ingredients for a meal so that no matter where we go, we have abstinent food that we can weigh and measure.

In addition to backup food, we also bring backup food scales with us. We never depend on people at restaurants, events, or other destinations

---

[2]   "GSA Literature." GreySheeters Anonymous. https://greysheet.org/literature (accessed November 15, 2020).

[3]   "GSA Literature." Accessed November 15, 2020.

to provide us with an abstinent meal. We are each responsible for our own abstinence. This is a commitment we willingly and lovingly embrace for ourselves, and in solidarity with our fellow GreySheeters.

Our sponsors help us figure out our own personal backup needs, and as we become more experienced in the Four Ps of abstinence, we evolve in our understanding of what is best for us. These are concrete details of protecting our abstinence, and yet there is a beautiful spiritual element as well. Planning and preparing our meals goes beyond guarding our abstinence. By removing any potential uncertainty about our meals, we make ourselves more available for whatever comes our way. And we are better able to be of service to those around us.

One member recalls her first week in GreySheeters Anonymous, when there were many terms she didn't understand. "People often said that such-and-such happened but thankfully they had backup so it was okay." Over and over, she heard members share about using backup.

After the meeting, she asked someone to please help her understand what backup means in GSA. She was taken out to another member's car and shown the zippered tote bag that the member kept in the trunk. Inside the bag was a scale, a tablespoon, a few small cans of non-perishable foods, a can opener, a knife, a fork, a spoon, and a few small packets of a GreySheet fat. This was an eye-opener for that GSA newcomer.

A long-time member shares that she always keeps two tiny backup scales in her purse at all times. In addition, she keeps an extra scale and extra batteries both in her car and in her husband's car. Her siblings live out of state, so she keeps an extra scale in each of their homes for her visits.

Another member plans backup for a variety of situations that might involve eating away from home. When he is invited to someone's home for dinner, he brings containers with each component of an abstinent meal so that he can partake of the host's food if possible, while being completely prepared with delicious backup in case he needs it. At restaurants, he finds that he can usually get what he needs. To make sure, he checks the menu on the restaurant's website ahead of time, or calls to ask if they can accommodate his needs.

When eating at a restaurant, it is suggested that we always bring a full backup meal in case there is an unanticipated problem with part of the served meal, and we need to supplement it with our own food. Also, the fancier and more expensive the restaurant is, the smaller the portions tend to be; we may need to supplement for this reason.

Some members make sure to ask the server for an extra plate for weighing their food, at the same time they place their order. One member shared that she usually brings one or two paper plates along to a restaurant. For her, this means she does not have to wait for the empty plate if the server forgets to bring it with her meal.

When planning travel, we make sure to take a backup meal or meals with us when we fly, in case our travel is delayed and we get stranded somewhere. We need to know what we can and cannot bring through airport security, and therefore what kinds of meals we can enjoy eating at the airport or on the plane. We then plan accordingly. We can prepare a compact but tasty meal to put into our carry-on luggage. Our sponsor or other GreySheeters who travel can give us ideas for these meals.

One long-term GSA member travels often to visit family both out of state and overseas.

> *When I travel, in addition to my small pocketbook scale, I pack two regular size scales and batteries in my checked luggage. When I fly, I always bring three meals with me: the present meal and the next two meals. My focus is on making the meals small and portable and getting them through security easily.*

Another member shares about planning her backup food once she's arrived at her destination.

> *I always keep things in the freezer because I never know when there will be an emergency and I'll have to quickly grab an abstinent meal and run out. When I'm sightseeing, I always bring my food with me. There may not be time to sit down at a restaurant, or to stop and buy what I need if*

> *I'm with a group or on a guided tour. If I am able to stop*
> *and eat at a restaurant, and I don't eat what I brought, I*
> *make a phone call to change the commitment for that meal.*
>
> *An important part of my preparation is always having phone*
> *numbers of my sponsor and other qualified GreySheeters in*
> *my phone and in my husband's phone. I also keep some of*
> *the numbers I might need written down and in my bag in*
> *case something happens to my phone. And I make sure to*
> *bring my phone charger.*
>
> *These things are the lifeline to my abstinence. And backup*
> *is not just about the food. It also represents my connection*
> *to fellow GreySheeters and my Higher Power. It's a three-*
> *way connection, because that's all part of staying abstinent.*

Be sure to check with your sponsor for details on how to be abstinent while traveling. Members of the GSA community have extensive experience taking trips within the United States and to other countries. In addition to speaking directly with other GreySheeters, we often use social media to communicate with each other about backup food for travel, among other topics. We can ask questions of members who have gone to the place we're planning to visit.

Those of us whose schedules frequently change usually keep a backup food bag in our car or at our place of work that contains what we need to prepare an abstinent meal. And some of us have food bags that we keep readily available in our homes, in case we need to leave quickly. For example, some members live in areas that at certain times of the year are flood-prone or have frequent wildfires, and an "emergency" bag is invaluable.

Our food bag may contain a variety of non-perishable foods, and also foods that will stay fresh for a while, and that we plan to change out regularly. It usually includes two scales (including one analog scale), spare batteries for the digital scale, a knife (a folding knife is especially handy), a fork and spoon, a bowl or two, a cover for the bowl, a spatula, and moist hand wipes. It may also contain a measuring cup and tablespoon for GreySheeters who weigh their protein, but measure their fruits and vegetables in a cup. Those of us who usually weigh all of our food may get our sponsor's permission to keep a measuring cup in our bag, but only for use in case of scale malfunction. Flashlights are also helpful for low light conditions.

One member shares that her food bag enabled her to stay abstinent in an emergency situation. Her husband was rushed to the hospital. She could not take time to prepare a complete meal, but she took her food bag with her. This ensured that she would remain abstinent, whatever might happen at the hospital.

A member with young children remembers when her son had to go to the ER in the middle of the night. She was grateful that she had a well-stocked food bag ready to grab as she rushed out the door.

Another abstinent member who has chronic medical issues keeps her bag near her front door. "I'm so grateful for the suggestions from abstinent members who came before me. Having a food bag ready to go means I do not have to worry about getting what I need." She has used it at least a half dozen times in the last ten years.

Whether we're in our own community or traveling, going through an ordinary day or dealing with an emergency, having backup food always at hand makes it possible for us to stay abstinent in any and all circumstances, No Matter What.

7

Challenges with Our Food Scales

Food scales are central to our abstinence, and to many of us they are even sacred. Yet they are machines, and therefore are subject to imperfect performance for a number of reasons. Keep in mind that patience and a sense of humor help when our scales don't perform the way we expect them to.

Experienced GreySheeters Anonymous members share strategies for dealing with a variety of challenges with our scales, and tips for preventing unnecessary mishaps.

If it seems that there is something actually wrong with the scale's performance, here are the first things to check:

- Make sure that the scale is on a flat, even surface.
- Check the feet of the scale to make sure they are clean and flat.
- Know that if the scale is on a tablecloth, the thickness of the cloth can affect the scale's balance.
- Take the batteries out and then put them back in again. Replace the batteries if needed.
- If you have replaced the batteries and still have a problem, check the battery connectors. These can get dirty, and they can be cleaned with white vinegar, dried with a cloth, and left for two hours to thoroughly dry.

Beware of water damage. Moisture can prevent a scale from working properly. If your scale has gotten wet, remove the batteries and place the scale in a Ziploc bag with rice, cat litter, or silica gel packets to absorb the moisture. Leave it there for one day and then recheck it.

Microwaves, cell phones, and other electronics can interfere with the proper working of our scales.

One member has learned that if she is weighing in the kitchen while the microwave is on, the number on the scale will rapidly change back and forth. She either waits for the microwave to finish or turns it off while she is weighing.

Another member needs to move his cell phone a certain distance from his scale while he is weighing his food.

On an airplane or a cruise ship, an analog scale (the type that isn't electronic) may be more reliable than a digital (electronic) scale, but it's possible that neither type will work at all times. That's why it is strongly suggested that even if we are accustomed to weighing all of our food, we should still take a measuring cup and a tablespoon with us on our flight or cruise, along with our scales. (Just be sure to ask your sponsor about the use of cups and tablespoons beforehand.) When flying, some members find that the best approach is to pack pre-measured meals. On cruises, GreySheeters report that while both types of scales work most of the time under normal conditions, weighing food is not possible on rough seas.

If you are planning a trip, be sure to have a detailed conversation with your sponsor about it before you travel, so that you'll feel confident that you can weigh and measure your food no matter what the conditions.

One member tells this story:

> *I went out of town to a cousin's birthday party. It was a catered dinner, and I spoke to the event planner ahead of time about my food plan. I was grateful that she was able to accommodate me. The night of the event, the waiter brought me a beautiful dinner, but when I began to weigh the food, the numbers on the scale jumped all over the place. My back-up scale didn't work, either. I thought there*

> *might be too many cell phones nearby, so I went out into*
> *the hallway and tried again. Still no luck. It might be that*
> *the electronic equipment the band was using in the dining*
> *room disrupted my scale, even at a distance. I ended up*
> *eating my back-up meal and took the catered food home*
> *with me.*

Even fully functioning scales can sometimes cause us frustration. One long-time member still laughingly recalls early experiences of weighing salad in a restaurant.

> *It would take me forever to get it right. I'd keep adding*
> *and removing salad ingredients to the plate and before long*
> *there were bits of salad scattered over the table. My dining*
> *companions were both amused and a bit frustrated. As was*
> *I! Over time I became more experienced, and now I just*
> *have a little back and forth with the salad to get it right.*
> *Sometimes I have to go a bit over the weight I need and*
> *then slowly take ingredients away until I get to the exact*
> *number I need.*

Tips

- Always bring a backup meal when eating out.
- Keep a backup scale or two at home and take an extra scale along when eating out or traveling.
- Always have extra scale batteries.
- Many restaurants have food scales in the kitchen. Some of us who have forgotten an extra scale have asked to borrow the restaurant's scale when ours malfunctions.
- Digital scales vary in the amount of time they stay on. We try not to get distracted and step away from the scale while in the

process of weighing, so we don't have to start over if the scale shuts off in the middle of weighing.

- Check with your sponsor about bringing cups with you to use in case of emergency.

One long-time member brings both an electronic scale and an analog scale with her every time she goes to a restaurant or someone's home. "This covers all the bases," she says. "I have only had to use the analog scale once, but you never know. And even though I usually weigh all my food, I bring a half-cup measure and tablespoon when I go on trips."

Whether you need help solving a problem with your scale, or you're simply frustrated, make a phone call. Other GreySheeters are bound to have a solution for you. We do not have to figure things out for ourselves. If nothing else, making a phone call will give you a moment to regroup and relax before you continue to weigh your food. We can make a phone call, ask for help from our Higher Power, and take a deep breath with a little chuckle to ourselves. How small these irritations are, compared to the benefits of weighing and measuring our food.

GSA Recovery and the
People in Our Lives

8

When People Ask Questions About Our Food Plan

Sooner rather than later, anyone who is abstinent on the GreySheet will get questions like, "What are you eating?" or "Why are you eating this way?"

When we are newcomers we may not be sure how to answer these kinds of questions. The reasons for our coming into GSA can be very personal, and it might take us a while to feel ready to share these parts of ourselves with others, particularly with colleagues or strangers. It is important to note that we don't owe people an explanation about why we are abstinent; all we need to do is focus on *staying* abstinent.

When people ask us questions, we always have the choice to simply request that our preferences around food be respected, without giving any details. If they ask further questions, we can say that we prefer not to speak about it. If they give advice or tell us their weight loss stories, we can politely thank them and then change the subject.

When we do choose to share about our program and our food plan, there are a number of ways that we can respond.

The first people to notice the changes in your eating may be those who are closest to you. It may be easier talking with them than with people you don't know as well. They may be relieved when you explain that you decided to seek the help of a Twelve-Step program. They may have been worried about you for longer than you know.

Some friends and family members might be skeptical at first, perhaps thinking this is yet another one of your many diets. (You, too, may have viewed GSA that way in the beginning). One GreySheeter in this predicament told us that when they started losing weight it became a little easier for their friends and family to accept the program as a solution. Now at goal weight, they tell people that if they return to compulsive eating, the weight will return too.

If your family is very curious about the change in your eating, you may choose to explain as much as you're comfortable with regarding your compulsive eating and our program of recovery. Start with some basic information, and add to it if they ask questions. Again, you do not owe anyone a detailed explanation. The people closest to you will get a better understanding the more they see you weigh and measure your food.

When those asking questions are casual acquaintances, work colleagues, or strangers, some GSA members choose to be very open and honest about their new eating habits and their participation in a Twelve-Step program. One member gives this answer: "I am a food addict, and this is the solution that has worked for me for many years." You may also say: "I have an addiction and certain types of food make me crave more of the same," or "I'm following a food program that works for me."

Some members explain that they have an extreme problem that needs an extreme solution. An analogy is that someone without cancer would not have chemotherapy, while someone with cancer would need chemotherapy. A healthy eater would not use our food plan, but we need this solution to treat our disease.

Since our primary purpose is to stay abstinent, and then to carry the message of recovery to other food addicts, we are mindful that this could be a chance to share the GSA solution with another compulsive eater. We never know who is struggling with food, or whether the person asking will later tell a friend or relative who might be a compulsive eater.

We are examples of this program; we practice attraction rather than promotion. For this reason, we try not to show arrogance or annoyance when answering questions about what we are doing with our food. The way we express ourselves can go a long way towards giving people a positive impression of GSA.

Ultimately, you are letting people know that there is a solution if they are interested. If you want to share even more, you can give people details about your recovery, direct them to the GSA website, and tell them about our meetings. You may even give out your phone number if you are open to speaking with them at a later time. However, it's important for newcomers to know that carrying the message about GSA often comes later in recovery, when we are more comfortable speaking to others about our food plan and our program.

Even some long-timers, when asked questions, choose to avoid giving any details about having a food addiction or eating disorder. One GSA member remembers: "We had moved into a new neighborhood and were invited to our neighbors' home for dinner. In response to their questions about my food restrictions, I decided to say: 'I have an eating disorder.' I could see they did not know how to respond. It was an awkward moment. Yes, the questions stopped there, but it was kind of an uncomfortable way to start the evening. What I learned is that—for me—it can be better to stay private about having an eating disorder."

Some of us who prefer not to share that we are compulsive eaters find it works well to simply state: "I'm on a special diet." Then, if people ask what the special diet is, we can reply, "I don't eat carbs or sugar, and I don't eat in between meals." If they want to know more, you can say, "It works for me this way," or "It's just what I do," or whatever feels comfortable for you.

Another way we can answer people's questions is by explaining that we have an allergy to certain foods and that eating them triggers us to overeat. Even if we don't break out in hives or have our breathing restricted, what happens to us when we eat these foods is an abnormal physical reaction. We might say one of the following: "I am trying to change my life for the better, and sugar and grains make me want to eat all the time," or "I am unable to eat certain types of food without abusing them."

Some of us jokingly explain that the "on/off button" for our appetites is broken, and the scale helps us know when enough is enough. This gives "normies" (people who are not compulsive eaters) an image that they can understand.

People often ask us questions while we're in the process of weighing and measuring our meal—which can be distracting—or while we're eating. We can politely ask the person to hold off on their questions until the end of the meal. Whether we're weighing and measuring, or enjoying our food, it's good to be free from a litany of questions. After we finish eating, if they ask again, we can choose to answer their questions with any of the replies discussed in this chapter.

> At a sit-down meal, where I am the only one not eating, or I'm eating something different from everyone else, I cheerfully answer all questions with, "I would love to tell you about it if you ask me again after the meal." Then I turn my attention back to my food. In twenty-four years, I can't remember a single person actually asking me about my food when the meal was over.

As time passes, we get better at deciding how and when to answer each person's questions. Most people won't truly understand compulsive eating, and that's all right. We are the only ones who need to know that we are compulsive eaters, and that GreySheeters Anonymous is our solution.

9

Dealing with Friends Who
Don't Support Us

As GreySheet abstinence becomes our new way of life, the positive results of our abstinence may be all the proof that most of our friends need in order to understand how important this change is to us. Whether or not these friends are aware that we had a problem with food, they are helpful and supportive. They ask polite questions about the details of what we are doing, and readily accept our weighing and measuring, our need to eat at certain times, and the fact that we avoid foods we used to eat. We can feel comfortable with these friends and know that they will never try to stand in the way of our staying abstinent.

On the other hand, there might be friends who do not support our abstinence, and might even try to convince us to go back to our old ways. Pushing us to have "just a little bit" of a food that's not on our food plan, they're upset when we decline. They appear to be embarrassed in restaurants when we ask for an extra plate, make specific food requests to the server, and take out our scale to weigh and measure our food. They don't seem to be satisfied with our explanations.

Why do these friends react so strongly? They may be annoyed with the fact that abstinence and recovery have changed us, feeling threatened by our obviously improved physical and emotional health. They might be going through their own struggle with food. Some of them are offended that we don't want to talk about the latest food trends and diets or visit the new bakery in town. Or they may miss the binge buddy we used to be.

With some friends, we can adjust our expectations and let go of our need for their approval. Or we can make changes in the way we spend time with them. For example, we might substitute other activities rather than eating meals with them. We might decide to stay in these friendships even if we are disappointed, or don't feel as close to these friends as we used to. Some GreySheeters relate that over time, a few friends who were formerly doubtful eventually came to encourage and appreciate their abstinence.

Some of us had friends who were supportive of our abstinence, but as we grew in recovery, we discovered other things about the friendship that no longer appealed to us. Talking in a negative and complaining way about food, diets, and relationships might have been a key focus in these friendships. When we felt miserable, we might have liked sharing a list of complaints with each other. But once we are abstinent, we gradually learn to be positive about our lives. We realize we have changed. Perhaps some of our friends have not.

One GreySheeter shared about a relationship she'd outgrown: "With this person, I didn't want to continue focusing on self-pity about my weight, my being single, and resentments going on at work. With the help of a sponsor I was able to let go of the relationship by no longer staying in contact with her. Looking back, it had never been a true friendship. We did not support each other. We only encouraged each other's negativity. It was a toxic relationship, but I didn't realize it back then—only now, in retrospect."

Most of us choose to let the friendship fade simply by not pursuing it. Another GreySheeter shares, "It's been my experience that if I do absolutely nothing to encourage continuing a friendship, it falls away naturally." This choice may be hard, but in the long run we will know we made the right decision.

If we are conflicted about how to deal with a relationship that worked while we were eating but now feels uncomfortable, we can talk about it with our sponsor or a GSA friend. It's not unusual for a newly recovering GreySheeter to go through this experience.

We know that abstinence is our most important commitment. Over time, we come to realize that true friends will respect what we do and will not try to sabotage us. If a friend cannot or will not support our abstinence, most of us make the decision to let that friend go and move on. We then open ourselves to making new friends—both within and outside of GSA—who support our abstinence and our overall well-being in recovery. Whether with old friends or new, healthy relationships are based on a genuine desire for mutual support. In recovery, we get to receive support and love from others, give it back, and cherish both abstinence and the friends who understand its vital importance in our lives.

10

How to Navigate Parties

Before we began recovering from compulsive eating in GreySheeters Anonymous, many of us used parties as an opportunity to overeat. When we were newly abstinent, it may have been almost impossible for us to imagine that a party was not all about the food, or that we could remain abstinent if we attended an event where food was served.

In this chapter, GSA members explain how they've handled parties and events, navigating difficult situations and staying abstinent. Here are their strategies, stories, and encouragement, followed by relevant GSA slogans. It is our hope that these members' experiences, along with the slogans, support both new and long-term members of GSA in staying abstinent without exception, one day at a time.

Choosing to skip events in order to protect our abstinence

In early abstinence, many of us chose to skip parties where food was being served. We were new and felt too vulnerable. One long-time member says to newcomers, "You may feel fragile and raw for quite some time. Maybe longer than you imagine. Please stay warm and safe and make choices that will make it as easy as possible for you to stay abstinent. You do not have to go to parties or events if it feels too hard."

In the beginning of my abstinence, when I was not strong enough emotionally, I would turn down invitations when I thought I might be tempted to eat compulsively.

If you are on shaky ground and are afraid you might eat compulsively if you attend a particular event, don't go! Nothing is worth it if you lose your abstinence.

Slogan: We Don't Eat No Matter What (WDENMW).

One member chooses not to go to events that focus specifically on food, such as cooking classes, or wine tasting.

I belonged to a book club when I got abstinent. It became obvious to me after two months that the members were much more interested in drinking and talking about food, than in discussing the book—that was true for me, as well, before I got abstinent. I made a decision to stop attending that book club.

I also skipped a big party and a wedding, in my first two months of abstinence. I just wasn't sure how I would handle it, and my sponsor said, "When in doubt, leave it out."

I did feel a little bit sorry for myself and called people to share my thoughts and feelings. Everyone said that I was doing a great job of putting my abstinence first, and they promised it would get easier. They were right.

Slogan: This Too Shall Pass.

In one member's first week of abstinence, they chose to skip a party because they felt vulnerable and were worried by the thought of all the food. When they first received the invitation, they let the host know about their food plan, and got understanding and support in return. However, in the end they decided not to attend.

Slogan: **Easy Does It.**

Making choices that work for us

We may choose to eat before or after a party, bring our own meal, or weigh and measure food that is served. Our choice mainly depends on whether abstinent food will be available, and our comfort level with weighing and measuring—or eating at all—at the event. Especially if we are newcomers, our sponsor can help us decide what to do.

> *Since eating together is a very social activity, in order to feel more a "part of," I like to bring my own food. I do that in most cases, unless the gathering is at a time that doesn't suit my meal schedule, or the venue is in some way problematic.*

> *When I skip eating at a party where a meal is served, I remember that I will not go hungry. Sometimes I eat before the event, or have a prepared meal waiting for me at home so I can eat right away after the event. Sometimes the timing of the event makes it impossible to gracefully eat before or afterward, for example, a wedding and reception. At those times, I bring my own food so I'm able to eat when others are eating.*

> *If I feel distressed, I create a pause for myself. I carry a "911 card" to use during that pause, or in "food emergency" situations. The 911 card has directions for what to do when I need help:*
> 1. *A reminder to ask my Higher Power to remove the obsession*
> 2. *A list of phone numbers of GSA members who are generally available to answer the phone*
> 3. *One or more GSA contacts that know if I text 911, it is a food emergency, and they'll call me if they are able to*
> 4. *The number of a GSA phone or video meeting that I could attend*

Slogans:

There Is Always Another Meal Coming.
There Is Always a Solution.

One GSA member was invited by co-workers to a huge feast at dinner time. They preferred not to explain to their co-workers why they weigh and measure their food, so they brought their own meal to the event. This didn't bother anyone except for the person sitting next to them, who made comments. The member recalls, "The best thing is, I didn't let it disturb me at all. And I loved every minute of that evening."

Slogan: **What Other People Think of Me Is None of My Business.**

(For a detailed discussion about responding to people's comments and questions about our food, see Chapter 8, "When People Ask Questions About Our Food Plan.")
We can graciously decline offers of food.

> *I say, "No thank you" when offered the foods I do not eat, or at times when I am not eating. I usually remark on the presentation and beauty of the food, since someone has put effort into the preparation. I can appreciate the item as art, even though it is not my food!*

Slogan: **That Is Not My Food.**

Focusing on the true meaning of an event

> *We no longer go to parties for the food. We are there to meet people, socialize, have fun, and nourish our souls.*

> *If I am in fit spiritual condition, and have a good reason to be at an event—such as seeing family or friends, supporting a cause, or spending time with clients—I go and attend to*

> *those people or that cause. I talk to people about subjects other than what's on the menu. I usually ask people about themselves, since most people love to talk about themselves. I remember that the party is about having fun conversations with people.*

> *I always try to remember why I'm going to the party. Is it to reminisce about or focus on food, or is it to talk to people, and share a nice time? I stay focused on other people, instead of on the food, or on my own problems and insecurities. It's also helpful to say a little prayer, asking my Higher Power to help me contribute to the gathering.*

One long-timer focuses on opportunities to carry the message of recovery from compulsive eating. When they take all of their own food to an event, they don't worry about what others may be thinking about their scale or their food plan. Instead, they focus on weighing and measuring their own food, or eating the meal they have brought with them. It is a bonus if they are able to help someone else by doing so. Even if the people at the event don't need GSA, they might know someone who does. (As we mentioned in Chapter 8, newcomers need not feel responsible for educating others about the food plan or the program. It can be challenging enough being new and bringing your own food to an event.)

Slogan: **Attraction Rather Than Promotion.**

Finding strategies that work

> *I don't hang around the buffet table, and I don't usually participate in preparing, serving, or clearing people's food.*

> *Bring an abstinent beverage with you to the party. There is often coffee, tea, diet soda, or seltzer at parties, so you might not have to use your own beverage. But it's good to have it if you do need it.*

> *We never rely on anyone else to provide food for us, even if they say they will. We always bring complete backup.*

(See Chapter 6, "What is Backup?")

Slogan: **First Things First.**

One member suggests the following:

> *Let your sponsor know about the event and ask for guidance. If you're going to a sit-down meal, your sponsor can help you decide whether you'll bring your own food. If you do plan to bring your own food, it can be helpful to let the host know beforehand.*

These are one member's favorite strategies:

> *I try to find a room or corner where there is no food.*
> *I suggest a fun game to play.*
> *I go outside if the weather is nice.*
> *I always keep in mind how happy, serene, and alive I feel by staying abstinent. I also keep in mind what will happen to me emotionally, spiritually, and physically if I take that first compulsive bite.*

Slogan: **Nothing Tastes As Good As Abstinence Feels.**

> *When I was a newcomer and felt shaky about going to an event, I found it helpful to call a GSA member before I went, and again when the event was over. That offered connection and accountability. It helped to support my commitment to abstinence.*

Slogan: *We* **Can Do What** *I* **Cannot.**

11

Keeping Non-Abstinent
Food in Our Homes

Some of us live alone when we come into GSA, but many of us live in a household where non-abstinent food is present. This can be quite challenging in early abstinence. Many newcomers say, "We are not far away from our compulsive eating days. How can we hope to stay abstinent if there is non-abstinent food available in our homes?"

If we live with "civilian" or "normie" family members, friends, or roommates, it's unrealistic to expect we'll never come in contact with their food in our kitchen or dining room. But with planning and preparation, we can make it easier to stay abstinent. This chapter contains ideas from GSA members around the world for protecting our abstinence when we live with others who eat foods that we do not eat. We also give tips for those who live alone and serve guests non-abstinent food.

Some members who live alone completely rid their homes of non-GreySheet foods when they become abstinent. In the past, they kept special foods on hand for "guests" who did not exist, and then ended up bingeing on those foods. One member recalls staying on the phone with her sponsor as she bagged up all of the non-abstinent food in her apartment and took it out to the dumpster. Others give non-perishables to a food pantry, or to a family member.

Other long-time GreySheeters suggest that we can safely keep food in our homes for guests. They note that visitors do not need much to eat. A small box of carbohydrates, kept in a cabinet we rarely use, can suffice. If guests stop in unexpectedly, we can serve these paired with an abstinent dairy protein and a plate of abstinent fruit. If our guests' visit is planned, we can buy food for them right before their visit and dispose of any leftovers after they leave. As with all food-related decisions, it's best to consult with our sponsors before we take action.

For GreySheeters who live with others, it makes sense to explain right away that we're doing a new food program. Depending on how well we know the people we're living with, we can go into as much or as little detail as we feel comfortable with. (See Chapter 8, "When People Ask Questions About Our Food Plan.") If our roommates or family members lived with us during our compulsive eating days, they might already be familiar with our history, and won't need any explanation.

It's easier to explain our food plan to adults and older children than to young children. Before we got abstinent, we might have shared meals or snacks with our young children, letting them have bites of our food or tasting theirs. In abstinence, our priority is to guard our food while eating our meals, by keeping our plates out of reach of little hands.

We can simply say: "No, this is Mommy's food," and move the plate away, or gently remove the child's hand. One GreySheeter set a scale aside for her child to play with. The child "measured" toys, blocks, or pieces of fruit. Those of us who had children after we got abstinent taught them from the start that Mommy's or Daddy's meals were off-limits. Our children grew up respecting these boundaries.

We take sole responsibility for our food and our abstinence, but it can help if the people we live with are supportive. Some of our family members were initially skeptical about the GreySheet—which was understandable, considering how many diets they might have seen us start and then abandon. But when they saw the emotional and physical benefits of our abstinence, their attitude often changed.

We have choices. Newly abstinent, we may choose not to involve ourselves with others' food at all. Or we may keep our contact with it to a minimum. If we live with others, we might keep our food separate from theirs, and prepare our meals at a different time from when they prepare their meals.

On the other hand, we may choose to prepare food for others. In fact, this might be a necessity if we are the only adult in the family. If possible, we have our spouse, partner, or older children help with cooking and serving meals, especially during our early days of abstinence when we may feel uncomfortable handling non-abstinent food. Later, we might feel more comfortable with this.

Most of us did not initially find it easy to juggle cooking family meals and our own abstinent meals at the same time. It helped to keep the meals simple. Sometimes the people we live with come to enjoy our abstinent food. We might find that, as time goes by, we're preparing less non-abstinent food for them, and more of our abstinent food for everyone.

GreySheeters have found strategies that can help us to safeguard our abstinence while preparing non-abstinent food. If we are eating along with our families, we can make our own food first, weigh and measure it, cover it, and reheat it after we've completed preparation of the family meal. Or we can make the family meal first, and then prepare our own food.

In the past, many of us tasted food as we cooked, but we learned that to be abstinent we do not taste our food until our meal is measured and ready to be eaten. To learn to guard against unconsciously licking our fingers or spoons while cooking, in early abstinence some members have used surgical face masks as a barrier, held a toothpick between their teeth, or worn latex gloves.

When we live in a home where there's non-abstinent food, we can reorganize the kitchen so that our food is separate from the rest of the food. If we decide to do this, it's ideal if we have separate cabinets or shelves for our own food. However, some of us have limited space in our kitchens and cannot avoid storing non-abstinent food with our food. If this is the case, placing our spices, oils, and other GreySheet foods at eye level means that these are the first foods we see when we open the cabinet.

If we decide to keep our perishables separate, we will need a section or shelves in the refrigerator. If we're lucky enough to have more than one refrigerator—for example, in the garage or basement—it can be easier to keep our food separate from everyone else's.

It's important to consult with our spouse, partner, or family before we begin the process of re-organizing. We don't throw any of their food away without checking with them first. They might actually want to help us with the reorganization, which minimizes our contact with their food. Young children can help by stocking their own shelves.

Some of us find a surface in our kitchens where we can weigh and measure, and keep our scale, cups, and measuring spoons on or close to that surface. Depending on the size of the kitchen, this might be a tiny spot. Some of us set it up as our space alone, so that others don't use it for their own food preparation.

Reorganizing our kitchen can seem daunting, so before we start, we suggest making a phone call to another abstinent GreySheeter. A more experienced GSA member—whether our friend or our sponsor—can give support and offer suggestions that make our task easier. Some of us stay on the phone with a GreySheeter during the whole process.

What about buying non-abstinent food for others? Sometimes we are the only person in the home who can do the food shopping. Before we shop, we make a list of what we need, then add others' requests to the list. We then plan a strategy for navigating the supermarket, which helps us to avoid wandering in aisles that may contain foods we used to eat compulsively. In early abstinence, many members make phone calls to abstinent GreySheeters when they enter the store, and when they leave. (For more details, see Chapter 5, "A Roadmap for Grocery Shopping.")

Our slogans may help us in the challenging moments in early abstinence when we are around non-abstinent food. One of these slogans, Keep Your Eyes on Your Own Plate, is especially helpful when non-abstinent food is in our homes. We still see the food, but we don't concentrate on it. This is a good time to remember the slogan This Is Not My Food. And There Is Another Meal Coming reminds us that soon it will be time for our own delicious, abstinent meal. Repeating these phrases over and over like a mantra may help if we feel particularly at risk of picking up a compulsive bite.

We can, of course, reach out to other GreySheeters in a number of ways to diffuse any difficult moments we have around others' food. We can make phone calls to our sponsor or to other abstinent members. We can go to an in-person meeting, get on a phone or video meeting, or share on the GreyNet. We can communicate with other GreySheeters using social media. We keep the slogan We Don't Eat No Matter What at the forefront of our minds. (See Chapter 18, "Without Exception and No Matter What.")

The strategies in this chapter can help us to deal with other people's food in our homes when we first get abstinent. Then, as our days of back-to-back GreySheet abstinence add up, and we are further away from eating the foods we are addicted to, we might re-evaluate our approach. But we always work with our sponsor to help us make the right decisions.

Protecting Our Abstinence

12

We Are Always Vulnerable to Our Disease

Once we get abstinent and months pass, our lives tend to become much better than we ever dreamed possible. Broken relationships often heal. We have peace between our meals. We might be more productive in our work and family lives. We learn that we can take our weighed and measured food on trips and adventures. Each day we are glad to be abstinent and we begin to experience contentment. We are reaping the rewards of putting our abstinence first.

However, our disease does not go away. It is sometimes said in Twelve-Step rooms that while we are working our program of recovery, our disease is "doing push-ups in the other room." For us, no matter how long we've been abstinent, we are still vulnerable to food addiction. One long-time member says, "From day one I have built a strong, safe foundation for my abstinence. But I am well aware that if I don't maintain that foundation, it could easily be destroyed with one compulsive bite." Many GreySheeters who relapsed after a long period of abstinence report that when they began eating compulsively again, their disease had progressed as if they hadn't had that period of abstinence.

The Big Book of Alcoholics Anonymous describes our disease as "cunning, baffling, and powerful."[4] "Cunning" means our addiction can trick us, telling us that we don't have a disease. "Baffling" means

---

[4] Alcoholics Anonymous, *Alcoholics Anonymous*, 58-59.

that it is confusing and frustrating. "Powerful" means that it is very strong—stronger than any human power. Another word that is often heard in describing our disease is "insidious," which means it progresses in what can feel like a subtle way, but is dangerous.

The disease can sneak in and convince us that we are fine. The only way to protect ourselves from this is to work our program *all the time*. This will soon become a habit, a new and wonderful way of life. Our whole program of GreySheeters Anonymous could be described as "building a defense against that first compulsive bite." As one member explains, "I try to stay safe by never getting complacent: I go to meetings, do service, sponsor, and continue to put my food on the scale."

One member had been abstinent for a couple of years and then went on a trip to California. She recalls that, before she even considered this trip, she started to cut back on attending meetings, making phone calls, and putting her abstinence first. Her life had become so much better in abstinence that doing these things had started to feel like too much trouble.

The idea came into her head that people in California are healthy eaters. Her next thought was that she had learned discipline in GSA, but she could now abandon her program and "just eat a healthy diet" like people in California. Initially she thought she would eat only GreySheet food, but not necessarily as described in the food plan. She did not call her sponsor or another GreySheeter to talk about this plan. On the first day of her trip, for breakfast she ate vegetables with her protein. A couple of days later she went on a long bike ride and brought a snack, which she told herself was okay because it was GreySheet food. Within a week, her disease had progressed, and was worse than anything she had ever imagined. She was eating everything she could get her hands on, and she could not stop eating, day or night.

We have a disease that affects us on three levels: physical, emotional, and spiritual. Our daily reprieve from compulsive eating is based on addressing our recovery on all three levels. Part of our recovery is learning to recognize and feel our emotions without eating compulsively over them. Many of us are especially vigilant about working our program and protecting our abstinence when we have the difficult feelings of sadness, anger, fear, or frustration.

It can come as a surprise that even when we feel happy, we need just as much—if not more—vigilance. Many of us have been raised with the belief that as long as we are happy, all is well. But, for addicts, this is not necessarily true. When we are happy, we can actually be especially vulnerable to our disease. Our guard may be down, or we may feel so good that we're tempted to neglect our program. We should never assume that because we feel happy, our disease is not active. (See Chapter 13, "Watching Out for Over-Elation.") As GreySheeters, we can stay abstinent despite our emotional ups and downs. Our program works regardless of the way we feel. We can experience all of our emotions, and stay abstinent.

In happy times, hard times, and ordinary times, our disease is always present even when we think it's not. Whether we are newcomers or long-timers, we only have a daily reprieve. We are still at risk of compulsive eating if we neglect to work our program vigilantly on a twenty-four-hour basis. If we stay close to our fellow GreySheeters and to our program practices, regardless of what is happening inside or outside of us, we can maintain our abstinence.

13

Watching Out for Over-Elation

Most of us wouldn't have reached the rooms of GSA if we didn't feel hopeless with food. Then we get abstinent, and some of us experience what is sometimes referred to in GSA as being on a "pink cloud." From feeling emotionally low, we can go to the other extreme, feeling emotionally high.

It is a positive side effect of abstinence that we are now present for all of life's experiences, and we can feel our feelings. We are cautioned to watch out for getting too hungry, angry, lonely, or tired. But as we briefly discussed in Chapter 12, we also need to be wary of over-elation: being so happy that we lose focus on our abstinence. One member told us, "Over-elation can be like sugar or caffeine for me. I want more." We may want to maintain, or even intensify, that high feeling.

Before abstinence, many of us associated joyful events in our lives with food, often a specific food. When we're happy, the thought might pop into our minds, "Just one of those (non-abstinent foods) won't hurt me."

As we know, normal eaters can eat any particular foods they want at events, with no negative results. If they eat more than usual, they feel full afterward, but they go back to eating normally the next day. For those of us who are food addicts, deciding in a moment of exhilaration—whether at an event or not—that it's okay to break our abstinence "just this one time" will lead us right back to misery, self-hatred, and remorse.

It makes no more sense to break our abstinence in a moment of happiness than it does in a moment of sadness, but the voice of our disease can be especially strong during happy times. We may become less vigilant, ignore the warning signals, and reach for something that is not on the GreySheet.

Over-elated, we can lose sight of the importance of working all aspects of our program in order to protect our abstinence, and the disease sneaks back in. A member wrote to us saying,

> *When I'm feeling great, I start thinking that this is easy. I can do it on my own. I stop making phone calls, I text my sponsor instead of calling my food in, and my meetings drop off. Then I'm surprised when I'm suddenly lonely and full of resentments. For me, to have a lingering resentment is to eat.*

Our sponsors can help us to safeguard our abstinence when we are anticipating a thrilling event. One member with four months of abstinence was preparing for her daughter's wedding. She was excited and full of joy, involved in the wedding planning and dress-shopping with her daughter.

Her sponsor reminded her that this was a time to make sure her food was prepared, and to take backup in her car to all of the appointments. On the day of the wedding, she was to savor the experience and enjoy herself, but also put her abstinence first by making sure her food was in order.

Sometimes the threat to our abstinence comes right after an experience of over-elation. It's not uncommon to experience a letdown when the excitement is over. A member with almost eleven years of abstinence told us this story:

I finished a huge project that took me four years to complete. Me! A food addict who'd had so much trouble finishing anything before GSA.

A celebration was arranged on Zoom for friends and colleagues to congratulate me and talk about the project. I was the center of attention. I felt so loved and appreciated. When the celebration was over, I was ecstatic.

I wasn't prepared for what happened next. I woke up the following morning feeling down, lethargic, and miserable. It didn't occur to me to tell anyone. I thought it was just a down day. But the next day I felt worse.

I started chewing gum—as much as I could, all day long. I didn't care about anything. I felt like I was on automatic pilot. It wasn't until the fifth day after the celebration that I began to feel like myself again.

I thanked my Higher Power with an abundance of gratitude that I was still abstinent. I hadn't used any of my tools. Generally, I have worked my program so hard every day that I must have had money in the bank, so to speak. I think that, if I had had only six months of abstinence, I'd never have made it through those four days. Now I know there is never a time not to be vigilant. We have a cunning, baffling, and powerful disease that wants us dead.

We have learned to be especially cautious when we are feeling extraordinarily good. The excitement of a job promotion, a new romance, an unexpected financial windfall, or a celebratory occasion can take our attention away from working our program; so can the painful letdown after a special event. Then the disease starts talking to us. We suggest you call a GreySheeter you trust before and after a feel-good event. At times when life is intensely exciting, go to extra meetings. Call newcomers and have them remind you what the first ninety days of abstinence is like.

Feeling great is not a reason to lower our defenses. We can be grateful for our good feelings, but at the same time be extra careful about our abstinence. Nothing compares to waking up in the morning and still being abstinent.

14

Anger and Resentment

We have already touched on anger in earlier chapters. But because so many of us have had difficulty with anger and resentment, we are devoting a whole chapter to this topic.

Anger is not bad in itself. It's part of being human. Anger about injustice, poverty, harassment, discrimination, and violence has motivated people to change the world for the better. This is a positive expression of anger. But many of us compulsive eaters have a history of either bottling up our anger, or letting it rage uncontrolled.

Whether we are in early abstinence, have been abstinent for forty years, or fall somewhere in between, we need to remember that our disease, even when we are not eating compulsively, can involve extreme emotions. Anger is powerful. Ignored, denied, or allowed to run our lives, anger can interfere with us working a strong program, so that our abstinence is threatened.

Anger is probably one of the most intense feelings we had when we were deep in our food addiction. Some of us grew up in homes where we were discouraged from expressing any of our emotions, leaving us feeling powerless. We may have lashed out in anger in order to have some sense of power over others—maybe the only power we'd ever felt. Then we did even more damage by turning our anger on ourselves, until we were driven to eat compulsively to relieve our emotional pain.

When we began to recover from compulsive eating, many of us didn't realize the number of forms anger can take, and sometimes we didn't even know we were angry. A member with almost forty years of abstinence says that she still has a hard time recognizing anger, until she realizes it's manifesting itself as deep sadness. In *Living Sober*, members of A.A. mention "Some of the shapes and colors anger seems at times to arrive in: intolerance, snobbishness, tension, distrust, contempt, rigidity, sarcasm, anxiety, envy, cynicism, self-pity, suspicion, hatred, discontent, malice, jealousy."[5] Once we realize we're angry, we can do something about it.

Not only did we not recognize our anger at times, but most of us didn't discover until we were abstinent for a while that fear can underlie anger. When we are angry, we may be fearful too. This is often fear of not getting something we want, or fear of losing something we have.

One abstinent GreySheeter flew into a rage at her husband for not doing more chores around the house. They both worked full-time, and they had young children. Later, she realized that behind the anger was the fear of having to do everything herself and becoming exhausted. With the support of her sponsor, she arranged a time to speak calmly with her husband and communicate this fear to him, and they were able to work on resolving the issue.

Life is full of times when things don't go our way. One member relates that she was happily working one day, when suddenly her computer froze. She tried to figure out what was wrong, but after forty-five minutes, she still had no luck. At that point, her frustration made her want to throw her computer across the room. She screamed at the computer as if it could understand her, furious because things were not working out the way she wanted them to. In the past, such an overwhelming feeling of powerlessness might have sent her straight to the kitchen to start a binge. Then she would have two problems: she'd be miserable because she wouldn't be able to stop eating, and the computer still wouldn't work. Instead, she called her sponsor, and

---

5   Alcoholics Anonymous, *Living Sober* (New York: Alcoholics Anonymous World Services, Inc., 2007), 38.

they ended up laughing at the image of her screaming angrily at an inanimate object.

Sometimes anger surfaces when we don't take care of ourselves in relationships. A member shares, "I can feel intimidated by people in authority. Often, I haven't set a boundary because I was afraid of hurting someone's feelings. I realize I'm not being honest with myself, and I end up angry at myself and at them."

A long-time GreySheeter was abstinent for a while when she began to get perspective on a significant cause of her anger.

> I realized that starting when I was young, I made up rules to live by—but I acted as if someone else put them on me. And I was angry all the time. I never thought to question those rules until I came to GSA.

How can we cope with life's problems without being consumed by anger? Our first action from day one in GSA is to eat only what is on the GreySheet food plan and nothing else, no matter what. Between our meals, we learn to live with strong emotions without turning to compulsive eating.

> In the past, it was easier for me to numb out with food than to feel my feelings. Now, with almost three years of abstinence, I'm beginning to allow myself to feel intense emotional discomfort, and I don't eat compulsively no matter what.

> I'm not going to eat over any of my resentments today. That's the beauty of GSA. We can feel, we can screw up, and we can learn from our mistakes—all the while weighing and measuring our wonderful meals.

As food addicts, we need to learn to express our anger in healthy ways. For some of us, if we don't, it can turn into depression. Our sponsor might suggest that we write down everything we're feeling, from start to finish, and then share our writing with them. Or we can cry, run, yell into a pillow, or pound on the sofa cushions.

A.A. literature suggests that we *pause* when we are agitated, resentful, and not sure what to do next. At a meeting, one GSA member heard the idea that for each year of our recovery, we are able to pause for one second longer.

> *A family member was in the hospital, and the rest of us were gathered in her room. People were talking over each other, trying to be "top dog" with suggestions. I was so angry because I couldn't get heard. I excused myself and walked in the hospital hallway for fifteen seconds, one second for each year of recovery. I remembered to pray for help. I went back into the room completely free from having to do things my way.*

We have found that pausing for even five or six seconds can make the difference between an angry response and a calm one.

Prayers from GreySheeters Anonymous and Alcoholics Anonymous literature can be wonderful for some of us when we're resentful towards other people. (See "Appendix: Literature.") One GSA member realized that she felt angry when other people couldn't control their behavior. Now she says what is referred to in the Big Book as the "Fourth Step Prayer" every time she finds herself furious at someone.[6] This prayer acknowledges that the person who hurt us might be spiritually sick— the same way we were sick—and is deserving of our compassion and patience. We then ask our Higher Power to save us from our own anger and show us how we can be of service to this person.

In the turmoil of anger and confusion, most of us find the Serenity Prayer to be very calming. Often the best we can do is sit down and slowly say this beloved prayer to ourselves. We can then make a phone call and ask for help in dealing with our feelings.

---

6   Alcoholics Anonymous, *Alcoholics Anonymous,* 67.

When we stay GreySheet abstinent and work a Twelve-Step program, we get to take a deep look at the sources of our anger, past and present. When anger surfaces, we can get support in a variety of ways to deal with this powerful emotion. And we have opportunity to heal wounds that may have been connected with our anger for a very long time.

15

Remembering the Worst of
Our Compulsive Eating

When we chose the path of GreySheet abstinence, we found a way to become free from compulsive eating. Whether we binged, ate constantly, underate, were bulimic, or were anorexic, we learned about the tools that would keep us abstinent long term. And there is an understanding among us: even when we've been abstinent for many years, our daily reprieve from our disease still depends on us working our program by using our tools every day. Keeping the worst of our compulsive eating history alive in our minds is a key tool in our ongoing recovery.

The quote, "Those who cannot remember the past are condemned to repeat it" emphasizes a universal truth.[7] We have a disease with a "built-in forgetter." We have a disease that tells us we don't have a disease. When we first come into the rooms, it might seem impossible for us to forget the devastation of our compulsive eating. Then when we become abstinent and start to feel good, the memory of the prison of food we so recently left might begin to evaporate.

But we aren't ever cured of this disease. If we think for one minute that we are, we're at risk of losing our abstinence. Remembering where we come from helps to protect us from the belief that we are cured of our

---

[7] George Santayana, *The Life of Reason: Reason in Common Sense* (New York: Scribner's, 1905), 284.

addiction. Sharing about the misery and despair of our eating histories with other GreySheeters—and listening to them share about their own devastating experiences with food—help us to remember. We are far less likely to return to compulsive eating.

One GSA member discussed his chronic relapses in his early days in our program. As soon as some weight came off, he would forget how truly painful his most recent binge was and begin eating compulsively again. Now, by communicating regularly with other GreySheeters, making program calls daily, and attending meetings and retreats often, he doesn't let himself forget. He stays close to his program and his GSA friends—those who understand him. He weighs and measures three meals a day from the GreySheet. Every day, he builds a strong defense against that first compulsive bite.

One long-time member remembers a terrible binge vividly, which she shares when asked to tell her story. After Halloween, she asked her husband to hide her children's treats. But later, she went on an hours-long search, found the hidden stash, and consumed it all. Her food addiction led her to do what she would never otherwise do: she stole from her own children. The next day she was filled with remorse, and also intensely sick with cold sweats and nausea. It seemed worse than any flu she had ever had. She also remembers that after a week of abstinence post-Halloween, which cleared her system of sugar, she began to feel better.

A bulimic member of our fellowship didn't believe she would ever stop bingeing and purging before she found GSA. There is one demoralizing experience that she keeps fresh in her memory. On a cold night, she walked from her house to a restaurant in town. She ate enough food for three people, paid her bill, and walked to the bathroom to purge. The toilet was out of order.

She began to take the path towards home but was in unbearable pain from the amount of food in her stomach. She couldn't wait until she got home. She leaned over and vomited in the road, immediately feeling horrified about what she'd done. Not only had she hurt herself, she'd also soiled the streets of the community she loved.

She now has long-term GreySheet abstinence, yet she holds onto the memory of that cold night along with her commitment to never return to bulimia, one day at a time.

Abstinent, we have a new lease on life. Abstinent, we can make choices every day. One of these choices is to keep alive in our minds the memory of the devastating experience of compulsive eating, and all of its consequences. We must remember the worst of our compulsive eating so that we choose to never repeat it.

Slogans to Live By

16

First Things First

First Things First: abstinence is the most important thing in our lives. This means that we always put it first, in every situation.

One member says that "not taking that first compulsive bite" is her top priority, and that her entire life is organized around that priority. She needs to Pray, Plan, Prepare, and Protect her abstinence before doing anything else. She says, "When I go to sleep at night, I know what I'm having for breakfast the next day because I've already planned and committed it. I've made sure I have everything I need for the morning—and often for the next few days' meals."

Many GSA members share that they always start their day by planning for breakfast, lunch, and dinner. Some GreySheeters prepare all of their meals at the start of the day, or the night before. They say that having their food organized is an "anchor" or a "security blanket," and allows them to relax. Especially when they feel anxious about having too much to do, the simple act of getting their meals together helps them to feel calm and focused, and able to make choices about the rest of their responsibilities. Others say that carrying their weighed and measured meals with them into their day allows them to be spontaneous if plans change. They can be flexible, and be present for the people they're with and the activities they're participating in.

First Things First means that we have well-stocked food bags available so that if we're suddenly hit with an emergency, our food is taken care of, and we can address everything else we need to do. First Things First means we take backup food with us when we eat at restaurants, events, or other people's homes.

The concept of First Things First helps us when we are planning a trip. When preparing for travel, we often say in GSA, "The first thing we pack is our commitment." The next order of business is figuring out our food for the trip. We plan ahead of time what food to bring with us and what we will buy after we arrive so that when it comes time to leave for our trip, we don't forget anything. Organizing our food first can diminish pre-travel anxiety and help us to calmly get ready for our trip. Once we've planned for our food needs, we can plan everything else we'll be packing. (For more details on emergency food bags, and backup food when eating away from home or traveling, see Chapter 6, "What is Backup?")

When we prioritize our abstinence and the program tools that support it, we can stay abstinent through any challenging situation we might encounter—including illness, job loss, the end of a relationship, or the death of a loved one. And putting First Things First means being vigilant about our program not just during a challenging time, but afterward as well. Newer members may go to great lengths to stay abstinent through a stressful time, but are not prepared for the overwhelming emotions that follow. Some of them have let their guard down, neglected to ask for help from other GreySheeters, and picked up the food—giving away their abstinence. Long-timers share that by seeking help from other GreySheeters during a difficult situation, and setting up support for afterward, they protect their abstinence.

A member shares, "During one six-month period, both my father and my father-in-law passed away unexpectedly; my daughter left for college; and we moved from one state to another due to my husband's job transfer. During these months, I made sure to put my food first. I always had my next meal prepared and plenty of food for backup. I also stayed close to my GreySheet community."

Clearly, First Things First extends beyond our food plan. Our food is first, and then there are multiple elements in our GSA recovery program. One member explains, "First Things First means recovery comes first, then life follows. I've watched too many people try to fit their recovery into their busy lives and then continually relapse."

Working our recovery program in its entirety helps us to be in the best possible state emotionally and spiritually. One member writes, "For me, First Things First definitely means prayer and contact with my Higher Power. Sometimes that happens on my knees, sometimes in my meditation chair, sometimes at the scale."

Another member says, "This is my morning list. First Things First means prayer and quiet time before breakfast, then sponsee and sponsor calls, then breakfast, then preparing my lunch and dinner, then starting my day."

Finally, First Things First is a useful guideline for life in general. It is a principle that we can carry over into many situations. For example, when we feel overwhelmed, it's enormously useful to focus on the next logical task. Remembering to put First Things First can help us maintain calm and focus.

17

Easy Does It

This chapter addresses the tendency some of us have to take on more than we can handle. This might have been true for us before we found GSA and, with our lives free from compulsive eating, we may push ourselves even harder to get things done, exhausting ourselves in the process.

The slogan Easy Does It is a reminder to slow down, take it easy, and let go of the intensity that robs us of serenity. On the other hand, perfectionism, combined with anxiety, can lead to procrastination. Afraid we won't do a task perfectly, we don't do it at all. In these cases, we are reminded of another slogan: Easy Does It, But Do It! We want to aim for a peaceful but balanced life.

The Big Book of A.A. says, "We relax and take it easy. We don't struggle."[8] This might take us a while to learn. One member talks about living most of her life in "emergency mode." In fact, many of us are still working on slowing down even after many years of abstinence.

When we first get abstinent, most of us experience physiological as well as emotional withdrawal, or "detox." (See Chapter 2, "Getting Through Withdrawal.") Going from eating compulsively to living without the physical and emotional crutch we were accustomed to can

---

[8]   Alcoholics Anonymous, *Alcoholics Anonymous,* 86.

be a significant transition. We might have strong feelings come up that we'd stuffed down with food. We might feel more tired than usual.

Eventually this withdrawal period is over and, with free time between meals, we might feel a lot more energetic than we ever have. But this is when we need to allow ourselves to adjust to our new way of life, and give ourselves time for physical, mental, and spiritual healing.

Taking it easy might mean that whenever possible, we avoid making major changes early in our abstinence. It is often suggested in GSA that we wait for a while before we start romantic relationships, change jobs, move, or begin any endeavor that will take a lot of time and effort. One member shares, "I was told that in early abstinence, whatever I held off on would come back to me. And it has! Relationships, graduate school, living in different parts of the country, marriage, babies, career, international travel—a whole full life."

Some of us think of addiction as a disease of "more." When we are no longer eating compulsively, we can tend towards more activity than is healthy for us. One member who is fairly early in recovery says, "God tells me to slow down, but I put my foot on the pedal. I want more money today. I want to work twenty-five hours a day and never feel tired."

A long-timer reflects on her early abstinence. On weekends, when she most needed to relax, she found herself painting her apartment, sewing curtains, exercising, and generally trying to make up for everything she'd neglected before she was abstinent. She remembers: "I had to make phone calls to get help with pacing myself. I rested periodically during the day. GreySheeters reminded me that I did not want to get so tired that I made myself vulnerable to eating compulsively."

Easy Does It helps us to slow down and also to let go of stress about our lives. One member shares a helpful saying on a bookmark that reads, "Breathe, my dear." She says: "This helps me relax and pause when feeling stressed. I can center myself, and let go and let God."

Some of us have a daily practice of prayer and meditation when we become quiet and ask for a Higher Power's guidance for our day. We then do our best to carry that out. As the day goes on, however, we may find ourselves trying to run the show again. We learn in GSA that our Higher Power is in charge, but it's easy to forget this when we are especially busy. At these times, sitting quietly for five minutes can help us to calm down.

We may approach tasks with impatience. We want to finish something all at once instead of taking it one step at a time. By breaking our actions down into manageable steps, we learn to create sensible strategies for getting things done. Instead of tackling a task with unnecessary urgency, we can ask ourselves, "Is it important to do this right now? Would it be all right to wait?" We learn patience, and to trust our Higher Power's timing.

One long-timer who was intent on finishing her to-do list found herself getting angry and frustrated that she couldn't do things fast enough to complete all her tasks. Talking with her sponsor about it helped her to pare down her list to what really mattered that day— which started with taking care of her food and eating her three meals. Then it was easier to prioritize the other tasks on the list, after deciding what could be put off for another time.

We do well to create schedules that don't stretch us to the limits of our time and energy. We learn to take on what we can manage without creating unnecessary stress. To our surprise, many of us find that when we do this, we're able to channel our energy more effectively.

Sometimes we make life more complicated than it needs to be. One member shares: "I'm the kind of addict who makes a simple thing very confusing, which causes me unnecessary stress. Soon I have a straightforward but uncomfortable situation coming up. For the next few days I will be praying about it, reaching out to other GreySheeters, resting, and eating the most satisfying abstinent food I can find."

Easy Does It reminds us to stay in the present moment. One member describes this aspect of her recovery:

> *If I can keep things in the day and in the moment, they get easier. I'm so often distracted by fears and concerns and planning for the future that I ignore what's right in front of me and needs my attention. I can keep things simple by being right here, right now, connecting with my Higher*

> *Power and asking for direction. And the direction I get at*
> *six in the morning, when I first make formal time to listen*
> *to God, may be different from the direction I get later in*
> *the day at work. I have to be ready to receive the "new*
> *memo" the update.*

Easy Does It can help us to be more realistic in our expectations of life, of ourselves, and of others. We can be more flexible, lovingly tolerate our own limitations, and accept people as they are. One member shares that family relationships have improved dramatically because of Easy Does It. She's learned that her expectations can cause her distress in these relationships. But if she accepts her family members as they are, instead of trying to change them, she feels calmer and much more grateful for them.

Easy Does It encourages us to stop and savor the beautiful moments in our lives instead of rushing from one thing to the next. Savoring our meals can be especially grounding. When we ate compulsively, some of us ate so much—so fast—that we never really tasted anything. In abstinence, with abundant and delicious food, we sometimes find it's hard to slow down and appreciate each bite. But, if we make it a practice to do so, meals become a more meaningful part of our day and we truly feel nourished. In our relationship with food, and in all aspects of our lives, we can relax, pace ourselves, and enjoy the journey.

18

Without Exception and No Matter What

In this book, we have defined abstinence and given many suggestions for how to stay abstinent. We use the slogans "Without Exception" and "No Matter What" throughout. We maintain our GreySheet abstinence Without Exception, on every occasion, everywhere, and at all times. We describe No Matter What situations as the times when it is particularly challenging to weigh and measure our food; or for one reason or another, it's hard to just put one foot in front of the other to follow all of the aspects of our program in order to stay abstinent. In many chapters of this book, GreySheeters share examples of weighing and measuring their GreySheet meals even when it was very difficult to do so.

Without Exception and No Matter What set GreySheeters Anonymous apart from other food programs.

We know that Without Exception and No Matter What are more than just slogans; these are words that we live by. Some call them our credo. Without Exception and No Matter What, when put into action, are powerful tools against our disease.

When we first come to GSA, we are told that we are addicted and allergic to certain foods and that one of the reasons that the GreySheet food plan works is because it does not contain those foods. We understand that GSA abstinence means weighing and measuring three meals a day, committing our food to a sponsor, eating what we commit, and not eating in between meals. We understand the need to be completely honest about what we eat.

But some of us resist when we're told that in GSA we weigh and measure our food regardless of where we are, who we're with, how we feel, or how difficult it is to get abstinent food. We might ask ourselves if we really need to go *that* far.

One long-time GSA member recalls,

> *I accepted the food plan, and I understood that I would weigh and measure my meals and commit them to my sponsor. But when it came to weighing and measuring my food all the time, everywhere, in all conditions, I thought, "Oh, no. I can't do that. Maybe other GreySheeters need to do that, but I don't."*

For months, this member did not weigh and measure her meals without exception, no matter what, and she was not abstinent. She remembers seeing the words "Don't Eat No Matter What" in large letters on a purple sign in the room of her first GSA meeting.

> *I would read it week after week and I heard other members say it in their shares, but I didn't really understand it until I finally surrendered and got abstinent myself. Then I knew that No Matter What meant I would never have to eat compulsively again. For the first time, I felt safe from the disease.*

Sometimes it is complete desperation that drives us to finally accept that we need to follow the GreySheet food plan Without Exception and No Matter What. One member who struggled with relapse for many years before getting abstinent said, "I had to be cracked open inside before that commitment could seep into my entire being."

The only solution to our compulsive eating problem is abstinence. In GSA we've found that along with our food plan, we need a reliable, unmovable defense against taking the first compulsive bite. Following the concepts of Without Exception and No Matter What provides that defense, ensuring our abstinence.

One GSA member says,

> *I cannot express how much the simple words "Without Exception and No Matter What" have meant to me in my recovery. Before GreySheeters Anonymous, there was never a birthday, Halloween, Easter, Christmas—or for that matter, a Monday through Sunday—that went by without me needing to eat compulsively.*

Now, not a day goes by without this member weighing and measuring three meals from the GreySheet.

Another GreySheeter relates,

> *All my life I was governed by my own insane thinking about what was best to control my eating. Nothing worked until I found GSA. Without Exception and No Matter What are fool-proof, ego-proof, and rationalization-proof. They are clear and consistent. They teach me discipline, conscientiousness, and integrity. They give me dignity and self-respect.*

In GSA, Without Exception and No Matter What are sometimes said to "break the back" of food addiction, barring the door to every excuse we used in the past to rationalize our compulsive eating. This is a tremendous relief for us, and exactly what we need in order to have peace around our food.

Before we came to GSA, none of our methods of controlling our food or losing weight could shut off the voice of the disease. It argued with us constantly, justifying our compulsive eating. The ever-present chatter in our heads was mental torture. We were powerless to ignore thoughts like: "This one time won't matter," or "I'll start again tomorrow," or "I deserve this," or even, "Who cares? I'll never stop eating compulsively, anyway." Now, if we mean it when we say we don't eat Without Exception, No Matter What—and act on it—all of that noise goes away.

We often hear at meetings that No Matter What means *No Matter What*. Even in the most extreme situations, we can stay abstinent.

One abstinent GreySheeter spent many winters on a sailboat in the Caribbean, where it was easy to get the food she needed. But on one occasion, she and her husband sailed on another couple's boat. She brought enough food for four days, although the trip was only supposed to take ten hours. When the weather turned bad unexpectedly, the group was on the water for three days and then stuck in port for one day, unable to go to shore.

The GreySheeter was close to running out of food, but the captain refused to let her off the boat. Angry, he told her there was plenty of food on the boat. But the GreySheeter knew that it was non-abstinent food. She retorted, "If I have to *swim* to shore to get groceries, I will do it!" Eventually the captain relented and she was able to get what she needed. In this unprecedented crisis, the words No Matter What and Without Exception helped her to be willing to go to any lengths to protect her abstinence.

Now, years after this GreySheeter first told her story in meetings, other GSA members still say how much it helped them. One member shares,

> *I can't tell you how many times I've thought of this story, and it's helped me to stay abstinent. I'd think, if she could stay abstinent on the ocean facing those odds, then I can stay abstinent on land in any situation!*

Sharing our No Matter What and Without Exception stories helps us, and helps other GreySheeters, too.

The phrase No Matter What is so integral to our program that we often include it in our communication with other GreySheeters. Some of us say it when we end a phone call, and we often add the abbreviation "NMW" to the closing of the emails and texts we send to each other. Many of us also include it when we introduce ourselves at meetings;

for example, one member says, "I'm grateful that I never have to eat in between meals again, No Matter What."

There are additional phrases that remind us how significant the concepts of Without Exception and No Matter What are to our abstinence:

- We don't *have* to eat compulsively, even if we want to
- We don't make any exceptions *ever*
- There is absolutely *no* reason to give up our abstinence
- It's not a question of whether we will be abstinent, it's a question of *how* we will be abstinent
- There is *always* a way to stay abstinent
- We go to any lengths to stay abstinent
- The debate is over
- We surrender

Without being completely committed to the concepts expressed in the words Without Exception and No Matter What, we can easily go back into the hell of food addiction. Fortunately, when we make this important commitment to ourselves and our GSA community, we are safe and protected from compulsive eating. We can lead a free and abstinent life.

Life in GSA Recovery

19

Taking Care of Ourselves

Is it possible to begin taking good care of ourselves after a lifetime of self-abuse with food? Absolutely. Abstinent, we now have a foundation for physical, mental, emotional, and spiritual health. We learn to reduce stress, increase peace, accept ourselves as we are, and let go of any doubts we might have about putting our abstinence first.

In early abstinence, there may be times when we can do little more than make it through the day without using food. We learn to give ourselves a "bedroom slippers day" that includes nothing more than resting and weighing and measuring our three GreySheet meals. Certain acronyms, sayings, and slogans provide helpful reminders to be patient with ourselves. HALT is an acronym that reminds us not to get too Hungry, Angry, Lonely, or Tired. Two popular sayings in GSA are "If all you do in a day is weigh and measure your meals, it is a successful day," and "If I put my head on the pillow tonight abstinent, I am a winner and a miracle." The slogan Keep It Simple reminds us that when we feel there is just too much to do, we can put our focus on our abstinence and our program.

Once we feel more solid in our abstinence, some types of change that are important to us may still come more slowly than we would like. Even with many years of abstinence, at times we fall short of our goals. Taking care of ourselves includes acceptance of our limitations and acknowledgment of our efforts. One member shares, "Sometimes I feel like a failure because I think I'm not doing enough, or not doing something well enough. At these times, I remind myself that I am successful if I go to bed abstinent. I can write down every single positive action I've taken in a day, and every simple way I've been of service to another person. I can choose to accept myself as a flawed but loveable person and let go of unrealistic expectations of myself."

There are times when maintaining abstinence is hard work, when life without the food is extremely uncomfortable, and when using recovery tools takes a significant amount of our time and energy. We may become exhausted, and even weighed down by the serious business of living. Deeply meaningful practices, rest and relaxation, and pleasure might help to make our hard work possible. And we are each responsible for taking the actions that keep us abstinent and well.

Weighing and measuring our time, just as we weigh and measure our food, allows us to take care of ourselves on a regular basis. A member with long-term abstinence prioritizes scheduling in journaling, meditation, and solitude each day. Another member shares that something soothing like a hot bath supports her when she's been working hard in her recovery. Many members find that connecting with a Higher Power provides a peaceful respite from hectic days. Those of us with many years of abstinence might take naps, watch movies, enjoy activities with loved ones, go for long walks, and include more music or creativity in our lives. Over the years, we discover ways of relaxing, and reconnecting with ourselves, others, and our Higher Power.

Some of us find great joy in our healthier, newly-capable bodies. We might begin slowly but surely trying athletic activities that make us feel strong, positive, and confident. We might take up golfing, dancing, and even marathon-running. There are GSA members in their seventies who hike and ride bicycles. And GreySheeters of all ages take walks for exercise, and to enjoy time alone or with others.

For some of us, guilt seeped in when we thought about taking care of ourselves. This was especially true if we'd always put other people's needs first. Slowly we begin to let go of our guilt. We come to believe that our needs are just as important as anyone else's. We begin to treat ourselves with the kindness we show to others. We stop trying to be "everything to everyone." Taking care of ourselves becomes easier.

We've spoken about some obvious ways we can take care of ourselves. There is another important way we can be good to ourselves: help others in the program by giving our time and effort through service. This helps *us* in addition to helping those we serve.

A long-timer shares:

> *One of the ways I have taken care of myself (and therefore strengthened my abstinence) is by reaching out in service to others in the program. I do service by sponsoring, talking to newcomers, and supporting meetings and the GSA program as a whole. Over the years I have taken on many positions for individual groups and for GSA World Service. Even when I first got abstinent, I could do service by arriving early at in-person meetings to set up chairs, and staying afterwards to help put them away. I was taught to actively pass on the program to others in the same way it was freely passed on to me.*

When we do service that benefits our fellowship, extend compassion to other compulsive eaters, and strive to be available to them as much as we can, we feel good. We may take the focus off of ourselves and our problems, and gain a sense of self-worth.

Being abstinent and taking care of ourselves in other ways improves our ability to help other compulsive eaters. We learn, as the safety announcement says at the beginning of an airplane flight, to put the oxygen mask on ourselves first before helping others with theirs. The primary way we are able to be there for others is by putting our abstinence first. We're also better able to participate in important relationships outside of GSA. Many of us experience new freedom with loved ones to have honest, caring interactions. One GSA member found that making new friends became easier and more appealing.

Over time, taking care of ourselves becomes second nature. We might try new activities and practices, and find which ones suit us best.

We might make these experiences even more satisfying when other GreySheeters join us. We ease the hard work of recovery, and in the process increase our health and well-being. This helps us to cherish and protect our abstinence, and supports us in continuing to give service to our GSA fellowship—which expands our own recovery.

20

Giving Up Harmful Beliefs and Ideas

Most of us spent years looking for the solution to our compulsive eating. We tried any diet or method of control we could find. Living in chaos with food, many of us had little insight into ourselves. We were sometimes unaware of the ways that harmful beliefs held us prisoner. We clung to them without even knowing it.

When we become abstinent on the GreySheet, we have the clarity to look at our beliefs about food, eating, and our weight. Some of us have held onto ideas that kept us stuck in our disease, or that might threaten our current abstinence. We can discover these destructive beliefs, and learn to be aware when they surface in our minds. We can ask, "Does this idea support my abstinent life?" If not, we have the opportunity to replace old beliefs with new convictions that support our abstinence.

We might begin the process of self-discovery by looking at certainties we brought with us into GSA, and noting how these have changed since we've become abstinent. For example, many of us entered the program so beaten down by food that we thought it was impossible for us to ever be free from our disease. One long-timer relates:

> *I had to ask myself, where did any of my old beliefs about food get me? I became willing to give up all of my own ideas and instead follow the directions of those who were*

> *abstinent on the GreySheet. Abstinence was a whole new*
> *idea, and I was willing to believe in it. Then I got to*
> *experience it for myself.*

Our experience of abstinence gives us hope and conviction that we can continue to be free from food in a way that we had never imagined.

Most overweight compulsive eaters come to GSA wanting desperately to get to their goal weight and stay there. But many of us thought that our recovery was *only* about losing weight. One member came into our fellowship thinking, "Hey, I'm a nice girl who just needs to lose a few pounds."

She is grateful to be at a healthy weight now. But in addition, as a result of staying abstinent she was able to learn that recovery from compulsive eating is about much more than being at a normal weight. We heal from the emotional, mental, and spiritual pain that we sought to escape from when we were active in our food addiction.

Before we joined GSA, a belief that trapped many of us was that if we just tried hard enough, we could eat like normal people. We watched them overeat or skip meals now and then, without suffering any consequences. We thought that, like them, we should be able to eat compulsively for a short time, and then return to normal eating. But we could not. Once we started eating compulsively, we couldn't stop for days, weeks, or months. or years.

If we were trying a diet or a food plan, well-meaning health professionals and friends may have encouraged us to eat foods that weren't on our plan: "Just have one. You can cheat once in a while." They didn't realize—and we didn't know or accept—that we were addicted to those foods, and unable to eat them in moderation.

One member shared that his brother developed Type 2 Diabetes as an older adult. His brother's nutritionist explained the dietary restrictions that were necessary for managing diabetes—but added that it was permissible to "take a break" sometimes and still remain healthy.

This worked for his brother, but the GreySheeter wondered, "What if I were in that situation?" In the past, he would have accepted the nutritionist's guidance and ended up eating out of control. Now, he rejects the idea that he could ever "take a break" from the life-saving food plan he found in GSA. "With the experience, strength, and hope that I get from participating in the GSA program alongside my fellows, today I know that if I 'took a break' from my GreySheet abstinence, the obsession and compulsion would return."

Before we came into GSA, some of us who were overweight held the belief that if we reached our goal weight using one of the methods we tried, we could once again eat as much as we wanted to, without any consequences. In fact, many of us felt that excess food was our reward for losing weight. We did not know that we were food addicts.

One member shares that, as a young adult, her pattern was to diet, lose all of her weight, and then immediately go back to her compulsive overeating habits. Of course, she became overweight again, outgrew her clothes again, went back to imagining that others were judging her for her size, and felt the accompanying shame and self-blame.

Many of us have had this experience. Our GreySheet abstinence is contingent on our solid conviction that even at a normal weight, we are still addicts.

From early childhood, most of us thought that the best parts of special occasions like birthday parties and holidays were the sugary treats and "goodies" that were available. We can rethink the deeply ingrained notion that celebrations must be honored with food. In abstinence, we learn that we can enjoy special occasions without eating non-abstinent foods. Instead, we might choose to celebrate the person, holiday, or event with songs, speeches, cards, and gifts.

A dangerous belief that we might have, even if we've been abstinent for a while, is that it's all right if we don't plan our meals ahead of time, or if we don't bring backup food with us when we leave our homes. We tell ourselves that we'll be home in time to eat, or that we'll have the opportunity to buy the food we need later, or we'll find a restaurant where we can get an abstinent meal. Any of these things might be true, but as we discuss in Chapter 6, "What Is Backup?" and Chapter 16, "First Things First," we never leave our abstinence to chance. The thought that our meals will still somehow come together—even if we don't prepare for contingencies—threatens our abstinence. The worst result of not planning is that we get so hungry or frustrated that we grab and eat something that is not on the GreySheet.

Many of us believed that we had to take care of others' food needs, but that we didn't deserve to take care of our own. In GSA, we begin to put our most important food need first—the need to be abstinent.

Before joining GSA, one long-time member always let her husband choose which restaurant they went to with friends, and what time they ate. In her early days of GreySheet abstinence, she realized that her husband's preferred dinner time of 8:30 p.m. was too late for her; and the meal often got pushed even later when everyone else ordered cocktails. In addition, some of her husband's favorite restaurants were not "GreySheet-friendly." She acted on her new, positive belief that she could put her abstinence first, and suggested that her husband meet friends for lunch—without her—at those particular restaurants. When she and her husband had dinner with friends, she found restaurants that could accommodate her food needs, made earlier reservations, and arranged for her abstinent meal to be served while everyone else lingered over their cocktails. Instead of being hungry and resentful every time she and her husband dined with friends, she put her abstinence first, and was able to enjoy both the food and the company.

As we continue to participate in the GSA fellowship, we can also move beyond examining beliefs that are directly related to our relationship with food, though they may have affected our eating. We have the opportunity to gently and gradually take a serious look at other harmful beliefs that may be based on fear, self-centeredness, perfectionism, or inferiority, for example.

Those old ideas often crippled our ability to be in healthy relationships with ourselves and other people. In the past, that resulted in emotional pain that could drive us to eat compulsively, again and again. We learn that addressing those thoughts and feelings head-on helps us to stay abstinent.

There are a number of ways to do this, including working the Twelve Steps, and seeking professional help if and when the time is right. (See

Chapter 22, "Professional Help for Our Health," and Chapter 26, "A Few Words About the Twelve Steps.")

In GSA, our abstinence can open the door to healing. We get to discover and let go of harmful beliefs about our relationship with food, along with other damaging beliefs. We begin to thrive. We find a new and wonderful way of life.

21

Dealing with Loneliness

As compulsive eaters, many of us were accustomed to being alone. We often isolated ourselves to hide our bingeing, purging, constant grazing, or undereating. If we were overweight, many of us were so ashamed of our eating that we didn't eat the way we wanted to in public; we got our food and went someplace where we could eat with abandon. We certainly did not want others to see us devour huge amounts of food.

Some of us had friends and families; we had jobs or attended college; we may have lived what looked like normal, well-adjusted lives. Despite our compulsive eating, many of us managed to show up and meet our responsibilities, at least to some extent. It might have surprised others if they found out that we felt lonely. But even in the company of other people we still felt that way.

Our feelings of guilt, humiliation, and remorse separated us from others. One member shares, "I was lonely in my disease, and in my shame about my body. Being sneaky about my food also contributed to my loneliness."

We came from the isolation of bedrooms, closets, cars, kitchens, bathrooms, and any secret place we could find to eat. We began to emerge from the seclusion of our own shame. We entered the light of GreySheeters Anonymous with the prospect of actual abstinence from compulsive eating. What a relief it was to hear the stories of other members who had done the same things with food that we had—and they were now abstinent. We became abstinent, too. We no longer had to hide our food. Our three beautiful, weighed and measured meals were out there for anyone to see.

But even though we were grateful for our new-found abstinence, some of us grieved the loss of our old familiar relationship with food. Long-time GreySheeters share that getting abstinent can be like moving to a foreign country: everything feels different, we might not know anyone, and separation from what has been familiar can be stressful. One long-timer offers this advice:

> *Go to meetings, meetings, meetings. Whether you go to an in-person, phone, or video meeting, there is always a way to become involved. Offer to do the meeting readings, like the GSA Preamble or the Twelve Steps. Share your day count. Let others get to know you, and you will gradually feel that you're a part of the community.*

Once we have over ninety days of abstinence and can sponsor, daily calls from our sponsees can be a bright spot in our day. Sponsoring not only eases our loneliness; we are also doing a service that contributes to the GSA community as a whole, and strengthens our abstinence.

Maintaining ongoing connection with other GreySheeters is an antidote to loneliness and an important part of our GSA recovery. One long-time member recalls that during her first year in GSA, her roommates kicked her out of their apartment, and she was laid off from her full-time job. She felt lonely, rejected, and lost. In the past, those feelings would have driven her to the food.

Instead of eating compulsively, she went to extra GSA meetings and spent a lot of time with other abstinent GreySheeters, both in person and on the phone. She talked about her feelings, cried often, and ate her three abstinent meals each day. Eventually, she found a new apartment and a better job.

Another GreySheeter relates:

> *Three months after I moved from the United States to Europe, I was so busy and exhausted with the details of moving and learning a new language that I didn't realize how little contact I was having with other GreySheeters, or how lonely I felt. Then one weekend, I made mistakes with my food, three meals in a row. All of my red flags went up.*
>
> *I called my sponsor, and after I shared about my food mistakes and my daily challenges, she said, "You sound lonely. What are you doing for meetings?"*
>
> *There were no in-person GSA meetings where I lived. My sponsor reminded me about phone meetings. From that time on, I paid much more attention to what I was doing in the kitchen, I regularly attended phone meetings, and I made more phone calls to other GreySheeters. And the feelings of loneliness passed.*

If we need to let go of old eating buddies once we become abstinent, this can contribute to our loneliness. In Alcoholics Anonymous, new members are often advised to avoid their former group of drinking friends. In GreySheeters Anonymous we make similar recommendations, since spending time with those friends can be a threat to our abstinence. (See Chapter 9, "Dealing with Friends Who Don't Support Us.")

We get to form new friendships in abstinence. We don't come into GSA primarily to make friends, but as time goes on, most of us do become close friends with other GreySheeters. And, as many of us become more at ease with ourselves, we're also able to make new friends outside of GSA who are comfortable with our food plan, and comfortable with us.

Some of us experience loneliness that doesn't diminish even when we are connected in positive ways with people both inside and outside of GSA. If you find that your loneliness stays with you over a period of time, despite being abstinent and spending a lot of time with others, you might start by talking to your sponsor or another trusted GreySheeter with solid abstinence. They might be able to direct you to other means of help.

There is no guarantee that we won't be lonely in abstinence. After all, we're free from the foods we're addicted to and our heads are clear. We are able to experience the full range of emotions, from happy to sad and anything in between.

In GreySheeters Anonymous, even when we do feel lonely, we never have to be alone. GreySheeters can connect with each other in many ways, beyond our meetings, phone calls, and text and email exchanges. There are events like roundups, speaker blasts, retreats, and gatherings, as well as recordings on CDs, downloads, and the GreySheet channel on YouTube. Members can access each other through the GreyNet, and various social media. See our website, www.greysheet.org, for more information, and ask other GreySheeters about how they stay in touch with each other.

22

Professional Help for Our Health

GreySheeters Anonymous, like Alcoholics Anonymous, supports its members in getting outside help when we need it, including from medical care providers and counselors. GSA has no professional affiliation, but we often exchange information about our experiences regarding members of the professional community.

For years most of us were steeped in our compulsive eating behaviors, and many of us come into GSA feeling broken—physically, emotionally, and mentally. We may have neglected our health during this time. Replacing our self-destructive behavior with taking care of our physical health might involve calling an advice nurse or the doctor when we aren't feeling well; having yearly physical exams; seeing a chiropractor or acupuncturist when we are injured or in pain; and going to the dentist regularly.

One GreySheet member binged on sugary foods before getting abstinent, and she didn't go to a dentist for most of her twenties and thirties. This resulted in some permanent damage to her teeth. As part of her GSA recovery, she makes sure to see her dentist as often as he recommends. Just as she can't undo years of food addiction, she can't go backwards and undo the damage to her teeth. But with abstinence, she now values and takes care of herself.

The emotional and mental aspects of our health may need professional attention as well. Because many of us in GSA have worked with psychotherapists before, during, or after getting abstinent, in this chapter we're going to talk more about therapy than about other forms of professional help. It is up to individual members whether they wish to seek therapy, and when. We acknowledge that there are as many ways to heal emotionally and mentally as there are GreySheeters in our community.

Some of us have never been in therapy, and maybe we never will be. In GSA, a number of us might even have found that many of our emotional problems resolved themselves through being abstinent.

On the other hand, we may have had years of experience with different kinds of therapeutic work, but it didn't help us overcome our compulsive eating, so we gave up on it.

For some of us, counseling was already an important part of our lives when we came through the doors of GSA. Our therapist may even have been instrumental in getting us into Twelve-Step recovery.

Newly abstinent, some of us choose to wait before deciding about, or entering, therapy. If we are going through withdrawal, we may feel quite emotionally distressed for a while before we feel better. (See Chapter 2, "Getting Through Withdrawal.") Although some people may find therapy especially beneficial during this time, others might feel that during withdrawal it's hard to make important decisions about therapy, or anything else

One member who had a difficult withdrawal felt bombarded by feelings that were intense and uncomfortable once she had stopped numbing them with food. "When I got abstinent, life often seemed overwhelming. I was confused about my feelings because I had no experience dealing with them." Most of that overwhelm and confusion went away after her withdrawal.

During withdrawal, another member felt as if she couldn't live with her emotional pain for even one more day. She wanted to rush into therapy to make her pain go away. But she heard people in meetings talk about waiting until they had gotten through withdrawal before beginning therapy. "I learned through experience that I *could* live through terrible discomfort and stay abstinent." This knowledge can serve us well both in our abstinent lives, and in any therapy we may do that brings up strong emotions.

Whether we are in therapy or not, if our withdrawal is emotionally challenging, we can listen to our sponsor and other experienced GreySheeters share about similar experiences in early abstinence. Calling and spending time with other abstinent GSA members often eases our pain. Their wisdom and moral support can bring us comfort.

For some of us—especially if we have a history of clinical depression—it may be important to seek therapy right away when we enter GSA, or continue therapeutic work we began before coming into program.[9] And several members share that if it weren't for their therapists, they may not have gotten abstinent in the first place. A member with thirty years of GreySheet abstinence shares:

> *It's hard to get abstinent when you're suicidal. It's difficult to weigh and measure your food when you can't get out of bed. My own experience is that therapy is what put me together enough to be able to get abstinent. After thirty years in GSA, abstinence is the foundation of my mental health, but this was not true in the beginning. And I've now sponsored many people who have benefitted from therapy either before or during the process of getting abstinent.*

We may gain clarity about reasons for getting counseling at any stage of our recovery, even after many years in GSA. Our issues might reveal themselves in relationships with others; maybe we realize that we're not always the easiest people to deal with. We may experience depression or anxiety. Or we might be ready to heal from childhood trauma. One member told us,

---

[9]   Whether or not they are in counseling, some members enter GSA and begin or continue to take prescribed antidepressants or other medications for mental and emotional health. These members are under a physician's care. Their use of therapeutic medication is abstinent, and their sponsors support them.

> *After some time in GSA, I wanted to talk to a therapist. The longer I was abstinent, the clearer I became about my problems. And then I sought out a therapist who was familiar with Twelve-Step programs, because I felt they would understand my whole being better.*

The honesty we learn and practice in GSA can contribute to an effective relationship with a therapist.

> *Before I got abstinent, I went to lots of therapists. I wanted them to cure me. But I lied to them—I never once told any of them the whole truth. I was too ashamed. In GSA, I learned to be honest by committing my food every day. As I progressed in my program, I was told I wouldn't get any benefit unless I was completely honest. I didn't die from telling the truth. In fact, I felt that I wasn't alone any more with the awful things I had done while eating compulsively. That experience gave me courage when talking to a therapist.*

Learning to trust and be honest with both a sponsor and a therapist can bring us an experience of peace and human connection that we haven't known before.

If we are seeking a psychotherapist, we can ask our doctor or people we know for a referral, or look online for practitioners in our community. GreySheeters may be able to give us suggestions, as well. Therapists can serve a role in our lives that goes beyond what GreySheeters, friends, and family members can do for us. Skilled therapists offer professional help for our emotional healing and for a variety of life challenges.

23

Letting Go of Self-Pity

Before we came into GSA, many of us lived in a state of self-pity. We were trapped in self-absorption, misery, and hopelessness. We felt that life was unfair, and that others didn't understand us. We focused on our own troubles. We often felt justified in this response to life, denying that we were in self-pity at all.

Many of us ate compulsively for decades. Our habits of pessimism, complaining, resentment, judgement, and negativity increased over the years. For many of us, self-pity was one of the things that drove our compulsive eating. Most of us continually asked ourselves questions like: "Why do I eat when I don't want to?" "Why can't I take the weight off and keep it off?" "Why can other people stay thin, eat normally, and be happy—but I can't?" and "Why can't I take a bite or a slice and then leave it alone?"

Then we come into GSA and receive the gift of abstinence, and we are full of gratitude. But when we find out that we need to completely change our behavior around food to stay abstinent, some of us find that self-pity creeps in. We ask:

- "Why do I have to prepare all of these meals ahead of time?"
- "Why do I have to bring backup everywhere?"
- "Why do I have to go to so many meetings?"
- "Why do I have to make so many phone calls?"
- "Why do I need to weigh and measure my food in restaurants?"

Many of us know the phrase from alcoholics in A.A., "Poor me! Poor me! Pour me a drink…"

Maybe we feel so sorry for ourselves for having to do all of that food preparation and program work that we decide we can do much less of it and still remain abstinent. Long-time members know that this type of thinking is dangerous if left untreated.

What can we do to help ourselves when we are abstinent and feeling self-pity? What is the best "treatment"? Here are some ideas:

Meetings

Long-timers say "Go to meetings, meetings, meetings, and have frequent contact with other abstinent GreySheeters." The clear, consistent message of abstinence we hear at meetings can usually change our feelings from negative to positive. We witness the gifts of recovery. (See Chapter 3, "Going to Meetings.")

Phone Calls

In early abstinence, many of us feel inundated by negative feelings. We realize that we won't always feel positive, that we don't have to *like* being abstinent every moment, and at times we might feel disgruntled or even rebellious. At these times, it's helpful to call our sponsor and other abstinent members. They might listen to us, remind us what life was like before we got abstinent, talk us through our negativity, and let us know that they have challenges, too. Most of us come away from conversations with other GreySheeters feeling better. (See Chapter 4, "Making Phone Calls.")

> *In my experience, making phone calls gets me out of myself. On more than one occasion, I have made a phone call and the person on the other end shares what is going on in their life—and it helps me to feel grateful for the life I have.*

> *Early in abstinence, I learned to make three phone calls*
> *this way: I called a long-timer, then someone with around*
> *the same time of abstinence I had, and then a newcomer.*
> *It was hard to stay in self-pity after hearing about the hope*
> *of what might lie before me, and about the misery of what*
> *I had just come from. And I had a peer to share woes with.*

Service

Our sponsor might suggest that as soon as we have ninety days of back-to-back GreySheet abstinence, we volunteer to qualify at meetings and make ourselves available to sponsor. We can quickly become part of the community by being a meeting leader or speaker booker. Before we reach ninety days, we can volunteer to read the GSA Preamble, Group Purpose, Twelve Steps, or Twelve Traditions, or to time people's shares. Over the years we have many additional opportunities for service, including representing a meeting in our region's Intergroup, or being on one of the committees that serves the worldwide GSA fellowship.

Gratitude

It may take a long time to change negativity and self-pity to optimism, and thankfulness for all that we have in our lives. Gratitude can often dissolve self-pity, and contribute to our transformation. (See Chapter 25, "Gratitude.")

Some people write daily gratitude lists and refer to them throughout the day. Others express gratitude through prayer, in the morning and in the evening before bed. Many of us pray before we eat our meals and give thanks afterwards. We learn to say "thank you" to our Higher Power for small—and big—things throughout the day, whether it be a perfect parking spot at the grocery store, or the resolution of a seemingly impossible problem at our jobs or with our families.

We want to create a new habit of thankfulness. We want to learn to think positively. A long-timer deals with self-pity about food by repeating to herself: "I had my share of those foods. I have given up my right to eat them." After she finishes each meal she says, "Thank you, God, for making it be enough."

Attending meetings, making phone calls, helping others, and practicing gratitude all work well to change our attitude. And finally, it can be helpful to remember that no one is forcing us to work the program. If we decide that staying abstinent is too much trouble, there is no one keeping us here. GSA will "cheerfully refund the misery" that we came into the program with.

We know that our shortcomings, including self-pity, will never be completely eliminated. In GSA we are not promised a perfect life. But we are promised freedom from food addiction, which enables us to take actions that diminish our self-pity over time. New, positive thoughts and behaviors become part of our abstinent life.

24

Insomnia and Eating Dreams

When we ate sugar and carbohydrates, we may have had no idea when we were tired or *that* we were tired. For many of us, ingesting these foods —sometimes in enormous amounts—either sedated us, or caused highs and instant energy, followed by nervousness, and often a rapid drop in energy. This was all chemically induced. Unaware that we were allergic and addicted to these foods, we had very little say in the matter.

Getting abstinent can be a difficult physical and emotional process. When we become GreySheet abstinent, our bodies are free of chemicals that have dictated our energy levels, often for years. Adjusting to this change may include physical withdrawal symptoms. (See Chapter 2, "Getting Through Withdrawal.")

Many of us are in physical discomfort that starts on week one of abstinence and that can last as long as six months. Even after the discomfort passes, our sleep can be disrupted for quite a while. Swinging from one extreme to another, we may feel exhausted and want to sleep all the time, or we may have trouble sleeping.

Being overly tired is a vulnerable and dangerous state for a compulsive eater. This is especially true for newcomers. As mentioned in Chapter 19, "Taking Care of Ourselves," we often hear this acronym and slogan in GreySheeters Anonymous: HALT: Don't get too Hungry, Angry, Lonely, or Tired. When we're tired we may lack the energy to do what's necessary to maintain our abstinence. And our disease can be stronger when we are exhausted and our guard is down.

When we are overly tired as a result of insomnia, members advise surrounding ourselves with other GreySheeters who can help us protect our abstinence. And long-time abstinent members have suggestions for dealing with sleepless nights:

- Keep "easy reading" books or magazines near your bed.
- Read program literature.
- Make phone calls. Join the GSA Phone List to have access to phone numbers of GreySheeters all over the world, who are in a variety of different time zones. This way, you will always have someone you can call, even if it's the middle of the night where you live.
- Get on a phone or video meeting. There's probably a meeting happening someplace in the world.

One member shares that she has memorized program slogans and when she has insomnia, she repeats them to herself over and over again. She often listens to audiobooks, meditations, or soft music on her device.

Another member comments:

> When I was eating compulsively, the middle of the night was "prime time" for eating, when everyone else was in bed. Now when I have insomnia, I simply stay in bed, or at least stay in the room where I'm sleeping. Sometimes I lie quietly and pray. I keep hot decaf tea or coffee in an insulated container in the room with me. I have plenty of phone numbers of GreySheeters in other time zones. "I won't die while waiting for my next meal" and "There is always another meal coming" are good for me to remember if it's hard to wait for breakfast.

After we've been abstinent for a while, we find that for the most part, our natural sleep rhythms set in. But for some of us, insomnia may persist well beyond our withdrawal period and beyond the other emotional and physical changes in early abstinence that can disrupt our sleep. Many people (not just addicts in withdrawal) suffer from insomnia as often as once a week, according to sleep specialists.

The practices that help us to sleep well on a regular basis are often called "sleep hygiene," and include avoiding screen time close to bedtime; having a cool, dark bedroom; and getting regular exercise. If our sleep hygiene is good and we have passed through the adjustment period of early abstinence, but we're still experiencing insomnia, we may seek professional help from health care providers.

While it is not our place to give medical advice, we think it's important to address the topic of sleep medication. These medications can be physically and psychologically addictive. As food addicts, we are vulnerable to forming addictions to other substances, which could threaten our GreySheet abstinence. If we are prescribed *any* drugs or medications for therapeutic use, we need to be very careful with those that have the potential to be addictive, or can alter our state in a way that could interfere with our abstinence. If we are so sleep-deprived that we are unable to function normally, and feel the need to use a sleep medication, we strongly recommend taking it only under a physician's close supervision. It's safest to use these medications only rarely, as a very short-term measure.

Before health care professionals suggest remedies for our sleep issues, it's wise to inform them that, because of the nature of our addiction, we do not ingest any remedies that contain sugar or grains. If we are sensitive to any over-the-counter or prescription sleep aids, we share that with them also. This informs their decisions about how to best help us.

Insomnia might not be our only sleep problem. Some of us have eating dreams. Like drinking dreams for the sober alcoholic, these are dreams in which we are eating compulsively—nightmares, some say, because they can be so vivid and frightening.

Sooner or later, most of us have an eating dream, and they are quite common when we are newly abstinent. We wake up from them terrified that we have actually eaten compulsively. But many of us believe that these dreams are a gift. Through them, we are reminded of the hell we left behind—without actually having to break our abstinence. Waking up is a huge relief, and we are very, very grateful. Even long-timers have these dreams. One member with many years of abstinence finds that having a sense of humor about them can be comforting. She tells newcomers: "Having an eating dream means you are really abstinent—if you were eating in your waking life, you wouldn't need to be dreaming about it at night!"

Our experience is that these dreams often come for no reason; we are simply compulsive eaters who have stopped eating compulsively. But eating dreams can be a gentle (or not so gentle) internal nudge to increase our program work. Members suggest that after an eating dream, we talk with our sponsor about whether we might need to review how we are working our program. Questions to ask ourselves, and discuss with our sponsor, include: Do we have a home group? Are we attending enough meetings? Are we making enough phone calls? Are we reaching out to newcomers or people who are struggling? Are we reading program literature? Are we taking time each day to connect with our Higher Power? Are we doing service? If we have ninety days of back-to-back abstinence, are we sharing our story at meetings?

For both newcomers and long-timers, having insomnia, or waking up scared after an eating dream, can be quite distressing. For those of us who have a history of eating in the middle of the night, it can even be a No Matter What situation. As mentioned above, we are lucky that there are GreySheeters—and phone and video meetings—in many time zones. When we can't sleep, we can likely find GreySheeters to talk to and be with.

Sleep is vitally important for our health and well-being—and avoiding getting overly tired protects our abstinence. But we need to be patient when we're newly abstinent. We can either have a hard time sleeping, or feel sleepier than usual before we develop healthy sleep rhythms. We learn that we can get through sleep difficulties and stay abstinent with the help of other GreySheeters.

25

Gratitude

Gratitude is such an important element of our recovery that when we are asked how we are doing, many of us in GreySheeters Anonymous will answer with a resounding "Abstinent and grateful!"—and mean it.

We are especially grateful for abstinence, and the tremendous gifts that result from it. Most of us reflect on how dire our situation was when we were eating compulsively and feel blessed by the peace we experience with food now that we are abstinent. We remember how isolated we were, and are thankful for the caring people in GSA who are there for us, day and night. A long-time abstinent member tells us that if she could take a picture of her heart, we would see how full it is with the immense gratitude she feels for the members of our program. She is delighted to have lost over 250 pounds, but she is even more thankful for the joy and contentment that this fellowship has given her.

Gratitude is much more than a feeling. It is also a practice. Our old habit of negative thinking blocked out grateful feelings. In addition, negativity can take the form of self-pity or resentment, either of which can disrupt our program and threaten our abstinence. (See Chapter 14, "Anger and Resentment," and Chapter 23, "Letting Go of Self-Pity.") In GSA recovery, we learn to pay attention to our thinking, and we have the choice to focus our minds on positive thoughts. Through consistent practice, gratitude becomes a new habit—one that we find is worth cultivating.

Gratitude can inspire us to take positive actions, and these actions can in turn increase our gratitude. One member who is thankful for what he receives and benefits from in his life expresses his gratitude by helping others. This is a spiritual principle that he lives by. He expresses his appreciation for GSA by doing service: leading meetings, sponsoring, and attending meetings to support fellow members. Service to our fellowship can increase not only our gratitude, but also our commitment to abstinence.

In Chapter 23, "Letting Go of Self-Pity," we discuss that making gratitude lists on a regular basis is an effective way to change our perspective for the better. Gratitude lists highlight all that is good in our lives, and include the gifts of GSA recovery, such as our healthy bodies, minds, and spirits; and renewed closeness with loved ones. We can also express gratitude for the simple pleasures in life such as a good cup of coffee, the sunshine after miserable weather, being able to walk long distances on strong legs, and other little gifts that we deeply appreciate.

Gratitude comes easily when things are going well, but of course hardships occur in our lives. We might lose a job, break up with a partner, become ill, or experience the death of a loved one. It might feel impossible to summon gratitude when we are suffering. We don't need to focus solely on gratitude when we're grieving or facing significant challenges—it may be that the best we can do is just to stay abstinent. But at these times, gratitude can be transformative, bringing us back to seeing the good in difficult life experiences.

Sometimes, gratitude surfaces naturally in the midst of our grief. One GreySheeter remembers:

> *When my father passed away, it was the worst loss I'd ever faced in abstinence. All the while weighing and measuring my food, I felt completely numb to everything around me. Then, at my father's viewing, gratitude broke through. Friends I had not seen in years showed up. Some members of my GSA group came, too. I was overcome with emotion from the support I received. Despite my loss, I felt tremendous gratitude and love.*

Some of us deliberately practice gratitude during challenging times. A member shares:

> *During a period of great confusion in my life, I woke up one morning feeling terrible. In my prayer and meditation time, I longed for my Higher Power to give me guidance regarding my future. Then instinctively I knew it would be better to write a gratitude list, and to focus on the gifts that were in my life already. I included my abstinence, my GSA family, and my Higher Power. I listed simple things, like trees, colors, and naps. I wrote down forgiveness, hope, and love. By the time I'd finished my list, my spirits had lifted, my body felt calm, and I was filled with hope.*

The GSA program gives us abundant gifts. Our gratitude for these gifts can be nurtured, increasing our peace and enabling us to fully appreciate happy times. During our worst moments, gratitude can provide comfort and restore our spirits. Being grateful can also make it easier for us to stay abstinent by helping us to stay out of self-pity and resentment. When we count our blessings one by one, we are transformed. And it is worth the effort.

26

A Few Words About the Twelve Steps

As we said earlier, this is a book of practical tools and is not meant to give instructions on how to work or interpret the Twelve Steps. We refer to "working the Twelve Steps," but we don't discuss them in any detail. It *is* suggested that we formally work the Steps, because this is a key aspect of our GSA program. We are told that this will bring us a life of joy and freedom.

Many of us come to GSA from other Twelve-Step programs and are familiar with the Steps, while some of us had never heard of the life-saving Twelve-Step programs before coming to GSA. The Steps teach us to live by spiritual principles. They are a guide to uncovering, changing, and making amends for the behaviors that have stood in the way of our recovery from compulsive eating.

The principle of Step One is surrender. Each one of us has surrendered to the fact that we have a disease and cannot heal on our own; we need each other, and a Higher Power. Many of us feel we are informally taking Step One the moment we join GSA.

Our sponsor can help us to decide when is the best time to start formally working the Steps, depending on our particular needs. Some newcomers benefit from starting right away, once they are abstinent. Sponsors guide others to wait, if they need extra time and energy to focus on learning the mechanics of GSA abstinence before taking the time for the Steps. Unlike drug addicts and alcoholics who simply put down their substances, we must plan, shop for, and prepare our GreySheet meals.

Most of us in GSA work the Twelve Steps, often multiple times over our years of abstinence. A majority of GreySheeters use the Big Book of Alcoholics Anonymous as the primary text for learning about and taking the Steps. We also use other books that complement the precise instructions in the Big Book. Two examples are *Twelve Steps and Twelve Traditions of GreySheeters Anonymous,* and *Twelve Steps and Twelve Traditions* of Alcoholics Anonymous. (See Appendix: Literature.)

We take the Steps in order, with the support of other GSA members, either in a Step-study group, or one-on-one with a sponsor or another experienced GreySheeter. (Although some food sponsors take their sponsees through the Steps, some do not; in that case, we find a separate Step sponsor.)

A strong foundation of abstinence helps us to deal with the important issues that we may uncover when we work the Twelve Steps. In turn, the Steps provide us with ongoing opportunities for emotional and spiritual growth, which help us to live a life of grateful abstinence.

27

Living Through the COVID-19 Pandemic

In February 2020, early in the writing of this book, the disease COVID-19, caused by the virus SARS-CoV-2, began to spread throughout the world. Our lives have changed dramatically as a result of this pandemic. All of us have witnessed our communities—and the world—in the midst of the greatest health crisis we have ever known.

In March of 2020, the governments of many countries made it mandatory for everyone but "essential workers" to shelter in place in our homes, to avoid the risk of exposure to the virus. If we lived alone, we were isolated from our friends, families, and communities. We had no idea how long this "lockdown" would last. People in most places were required to wear face masks if it was necessary to leave the house. Everyone was asked to practice "social distancing" or "physical distancing" by staying at least six feet away from people who weren't in our households.

If we were essential workers, like medical personnel, grocery store workers, or delivery drivers, we risked contracting the virus and had to take extra precautions to avoid exposing our families.

We saw the damage COVID-19 caused to those who were afflicted and their families. People we knew and loved fell victim to the disease, and we were devastated when some of them lost their lives.

Businesses of many types were closed down. We witnessed a dramatic downturn of the world's economies. The United States experienced the worst financial crisis since the Great Depression in 1929. In some countries, the economic crisis was the worst in their entire history.

Many of us lost our jobs or our businesses. Our work may have slowed down significantly, or become much more intense. Some of us had to reinvent the way we worked in order to work online from home.

Schools were shut down, so some of us became teachers to the children in our families, learning along with them how to access virtual educational forums. As students struggled with online learning, school districts worldwide grappled with decisions about opening schools again, even when they were allowed to. The priority was keeping students safe from the threat of contagion.

At the beginning of the pandemic, as COVID-19 spread and governments issued shelter-in-place orders, many people panicked. They ran to grocery stores and pharmacies, stocking up on everything they might or might not need. For the first couple of weeks, the items we wanted were not always available.

Not surprisingly, we heard that many GreySheeters, when asked how they were doing, responded that because GSA had trained them so well to Pray, Plan, Prepare, and Protect their abstinence, they felt safe. They reported that in spite of the initial anxiety caused by the onset of the pandemic and the wait for protocol instructions, they felt comfortable regarding their food. They had plenty of the food in their homes—enough to last until they could go shopping again.

In some parts of the world, people who had contact with someone with COVID-19 were required to quarantine themselves for seven to fourteen days. They couldn't leave their homes for any reason. Some quarantined GreySheeters used online grocery shopping services. Others asked family members or friends to shop for them.

From the beginning of the pandemic, the places where groups could gather for meetings closed down. While many people worldwide had a hard time learning to use video conferencing platforms, GreySheeters continued to attend our smoothly run, regular video meetings—and we easily transformed many of our in-person meetings into online meetings.

Even those of us who were new to video conferencing gave it a try and adjusted quickly. People who hadn't seen each other for years were now frequenting the same online meetings. Sponsors and sponsees who did not live near each other were able to "meet" for the first time. In addition to multiple daily video meetings, all of the regular GSA phone meetings were available to us.

Many of us felt profoundly grateful when we realized how our GSA experience prepared us for staying safe during the pandemic. As addicts, in the past we might have been the kind of people who thought we knew better than the experts. Maybe we fought authority, and tried to be self-sufficient—even though every single time we tried, we failed. To get and stay abstinent, most of us first had to accept that we had a deadly disease. We had to surrender everything we thought we knew about food and follow the guidance of our sponsors. We learned a valuable lesson in GSA: to be safe from a deadly illness, trust the experts and do what they tell you to do.

At the start of the pandemic, we were told there was a virus that knew no boundaries, would invade every country, and caused a disease that could be fatal. Most GreySheeters did not question what the experts told us about how to protect ourselves from the virus. We followed their directions.

Some abstinent members shared that, if they had been eating compulsively during this pandemic, they would have gone out often to find food despite orders to stay at home. If they had been active in their addiction, they would have placed themselves and others at risk.

Our experience in GSA helped us deal with the pandemic in an additional way. When we were newly abstinent GreySheeters, most of us experienced not knowing what would come next, and then found our footing and settled into that new abstinent life. When the pandemic began, we knew what it felt like to be lost in a brand-new world. And then we were able to adjust to the "new normal."

Now, well into the pandemic, it's easy for us to feel connected to other GreySheeters, even though we are physically separated from each other. We continue to meet daily on video and phone meetings. In between meetings, we stay in touch through our phones and computers. We tell each other how it feels to live with the losses and challenges associated with the pandemic. We share about our fears, and about the stress of keeping safe. We talk about how hard it is, wondering if we might go into another lockdown. Members express tremendous gratitude for our recovery and for our meetings; in fact, as the pandemic continues, gratitude is the primary tool most of us are using on a daily basis to cope.

During this time, it is an extraordinary gift to be a part of the GSA community. And we've been able to provide a good example to others of how to walk through a crisis, staying connected with others, one day at a time.

The COVID-19 pandemic might be the most difficult and Long lasting No Matter What that some GreySheeters have ever gone through. It is a testament to the power of GSA that so many GreySheeters are staying abstinent through the pandemic. And our numbers are growing as people in trouble with food attend our meetings and witness the recovery and the relief from food addiction that our members have experienced.

Appendix

Literature

Practicing the GreySheeters Anonymous program fully means incorporating into our lives all of the tools and strategies that are part of this recovery path we have chosen. We actively embrace and follow the GSA food plan. We work the Steps and practice their principles in our daily lives. We attend meetings, connect with fellow GSA members, and carry the message of recovery to still suffering compulsive eaters. And we read Conference-Approved Literature that supports our recovery. (See www.greysheet.org for an explanation of Conference-Approved Literature.)

Our GSA fellowship is relatively new, and much of our literature is yet to be written. We look forward to adding to our offerings over time. Still, there are already valuable GSA materials to choose from. In addition, we use literature from Alcoholics Anonymous.

Each of us can find literature that we connect with, and our favorite literature is well worth rereading frequently. A longtime member shared that she has read one of her favorite pieces of literature too many times to count. Each time she rereads certain passages, even those she knows by heart, she feels as if she's reading them for the first time. She finds a new, deeper meaning.

Here are some Conference-Approved books and pamphlets to help us understand ourselves, our program, our fellows, and our journey of recovery.

Alcoholics Anonymous

This is the original text of A.A.'s Twelve-Step program of recovery. It was written and published in 1939 by the A.A. members who first attained sobriety in the 1930s. It is affectionately called The Big Book. There is much wisdom in this text. There are precise instructions for how to take the Twelve Steps of recovery. Alcoholics Anonymous is the parent program of GreySheeters Anonymous. We are guided by A.A. and have no affiliation with other Twelve-Step programs for food addiction.

Twelve Steps and Twelve Traditions

Usually referred to as "The A.A. Twelve and Twelve," this book was originally written in installments for the *A.A. Grapevine* newsletter. It serves as a companion to the Big Book for further explanation of the Twelve Steps. It also contains both the short and long forms of the Twelve Traditions. The Steps and Traditions give us strategies and principles to guide our own recovery, our relationships with others, and our participation in our Twelve Step groups.

Twelve Steps and Twelve Traditions of GreySheeters Anonymous

This is GSA's first book, published in 2015. Members usually refer to it as "The GSA Twelve and Twelve" to distinguish it from A.A.'s *Twelve Steps and Twelve Traditions.* As in the A.A. Twelve and Twelve, the chapters are organized around the Twelve Steps and Twelve Traditions. It presents ways of implementing the program to support long-term abstinence from compulsive eating.

The GreySheet Food Plan

The GreySheeters Anonymous food plan, printed on grey paper, is a basic guide for sponsors and sponsees on the nuts and bolts of the GSA food plan. It includes the list of abstinent foods, a guide to portions, and some explanations and inspiration to support our commitment to abstinence. The food plan comes with a sponsor. Qualified sponsors can get copies for their sponsees from their Intergroup Service Representative.

The GreySheet is being translated into many other languages for GreySheeters all over the world.

The GSA Website

Our website, www.greysheet.org, is full of helpful literature and news about our fellowship. You can also find printable short-form literature such as:

- *A Solution for Compulsive Eaters*
- *GreySheet Definitions and Slogans*
- *Journey into Daylight: Escaping from the Fist of Food* (Written for Youth)
- *If You Are a Healthcare Professional*
- *FAQs for Newcomers* (Fall 2021).

Service Matters

This is GSA's monthly online newsletter about service. Each issue contains upcoming GSA events, reports from the different World Service Conference Committees, the Board of Trustees column, and available service opportunities. You can read Service Matters on the www.greysheet.org website and sign up there to receive it by email.

Printed in Great Britain
by Amazon